THE PEOPLE LOOK AT RADIO

The People Look at
RADIO

Report on a survey conducted by
THE NATIONAL OPINION RESEARCH CENTER
University of Denver
HARRY FIELD, *Director*

Analyzed and interpreted by the
BUREAU OF APPLIED SOCIAL RESEARCH
Columbia University
PAUL F. LAZARSFELD, *Director*

Chapel Hill
THE UNIVERSITY OF NORTH CAROLINA PRESS

Copyright, 1946, by
The University of North Carolina Press

PRINTED IN THE UNITED STATES OF AMERICA BY
WILLIAM BYRD PRESS • RICHMOND

CONTENTS

CHAPTER	PAGE
PREFACE	vii

I. THE SCORE CARD 3
    Overall Appraisal
    Annoyances and Dissatisfactions

II. ADVERTISING 13
    The Description of an Attitude
    Why Should Anyone Like Commercials?
    Danger Signals
    What's Wrong with Commercials
        (a) Volume and Position
        (b) Uninteresting Content
        (c) Overselling
        (d) Violation of Taboos
        (e) Attention-getting Devices
    What Should Be Done about Commercials

III. RADIO FOR WHAT? 38
    The Broadcasters' Dilemma
    News Programs
    Comedy Variety Shows
    Music
    Daytime Serials
    Learning from the Radio
        Forums
        Quiz Programs
        Religious Programs

IV. THE CRITIC, THE PEOPLE AND THE INDUSTRY 65
    Social Stratification and Criticism
    The Role of the Broadcaster

CONTENTS—CONTINUED

    The Five Pillars of Radio Criticism
        (a) Advertising
        (b) Radio as an Educational Device
        (c) Access to the Air
        (d) Artistic Considerations
        (e) The Problem of Social Significance
    Areas of Ignorance
    The Role of the Government

APPENDIX

A. CHARACTERISTICS OF THE SAMPLE 93

B. QUESTIONNAIRE AND RESULTS 99

C. SUPPLEMENTARY SAMPLES 117

D. APPENDIX TABLES 122

PREFACE

IN JUNE, 1943, THE NATIONAL ASSOCIATION OF Broadcasters planned a national survey of the public's understanding and acceptance of radio in the United States. The object was to assess the strengths and weaknesses of the radio industry, to ascertain where radio stands with the public, in order to blueprint a sound plan of action for the future of broadcasting.

Exigencies of the war postponed the project until November, 1945, when the NAB commissioned the University of Denver's National Opinion Research Center to carry through this first nationwide investigation of the public's attitudes toward radio.[1] Columbia University's Bureau of Applied Social Research subsequently was asked to cooperate in the analysis and interpretation of the findings of the survey which are reported here. Credit for the careful planning of the study and working out of the questionnaire belongs to the NAB and the National Opinion Research Center.

The generally favorable attitude of the American public toward existing radio is brought out in the first chapter. This should come as no surprise to anyone who has given even superficial thought to the radio scene in this country. The average man listens to the radio almost three hours and the average woman listens almost four hours a day to the radio. It is not conceivable that people will spend hundreds of hours of their leisure time on something which they do not enjoy. If the sponsors of this study had been satisfied to show that people like radio very much, their case might be amply proved from these findings.

But the scope of the study was much broader. The second

---

1. Details on the methods used in the survey are given in Appendix A; the questionnaire and results are shown in Appendix B.

chapter, for example, reports in detail what people had to say on the topic of advertising. The questionnaire underlying the study asked a number of questions which probed into the matter from all sides. The results are of two kinds.

The findings show that only a third of the people interviewed have an unfavorable attitude toward advertising. This result will come as a surprise to many readers, even though students of the matter may have expected it. We all have a tendency to assume that everyone reacts as we ourselves do. But one of the merits of this kind of research is the fact that it brings out the voice of that large majority of the people who do not write letters to editors and who do not participate in discussions in women's clubs.

In the same chapter in which this general attitude toward advertising is shown, the criticism of the minority is given a thorough airing. There is, to our knowledge, no other study on record where an industry has on its own initiative presented the argument of its critics as fully and as frankly as it is done in the present report.

The third chapter uses the findings of the survey to point up some of the complex problems with which radio programming is faced. For different groups of the population radio has quite different functions; group tastes and their expectations vary much more than the ordinary listener, and very often the individual broadcaster, is aware. For the reader who is new to the study of radio as a social institution, this chapter should be a revealing introduction.

Throughout the report, stress is laid on the limitations as well as on the merits of this kind of investigation. While public satisfaction is a very important criterion, it is only one of several which should be applied to the evaluation of radio's performance. The intrinsic merit of programs and the social implication of their development within the framework of American radio must also be considered. The fourth chapter deals with the question of criticism in its larger context and shows some of the problems which radio will have to face in the future. The findings of the survey, while they will give pride to the broadcasters for their past performance, are here used to stress the social responsibility of radio and to point out areas of desirable improvement.

Thus the study has brought out two things. On the one hand, it has shown that the large majority of the people in this country are pleased with radio as it is. On the other hand, the voice of the critical minority has been given a hearing. The fact that the National Association of Broadcasters sought out independent research experts to prepare and report such a survey is a sign that the industry is doing its best to mold a constructive program of action from the great variety of forces which impinge upon it. And it is encouraging also that the NAB conceives of this survey as the first of a series of continuing studies.

PAUL F. LAZARSFELD

THE PEOPLE LOOK AT RADIO

Chapter I. THE SCORE CARD

How can a social institution, like radio, be truly evaluated as to its present performance? What type or types of yardsticks can be successfully used?

At first glance, it might seem that in a democracy a public opinion survey would not only be a good but also a sufficient measure. But reflection indicates that while opinion surveys are one of the essential tools, they cannot stand alone. At least two other methods for evaluating any institution have to be taken into account.

One obvious approach is to see whether the product lives up to a high standard. Whether it be an automobile, a can of soup, or a program schedule, there are measures by which performances can be gauged. These are different for different products. In an automobile, it is efficiency and reliability; in a soup, it is taste and purity. What is it for radio programs? Quite a number of criteria are essential for the adequate evaluation of radio: Are the programs diversified enough to satisfy different groups in the population? How many of them live up to the aesthetic standards on which experts can agree? How much do they conform to the tastes and values prevailing in the American community? Is there a spirit of experimentation and a drive for self-improvement noticeable in the whole program fare?

It is often difficult to reconcile such standards. Radio is expected to be impartial in its reporting of news and public affairs. It should give time for the expression of the ideas of minorities and even of extremists. But when does impartiality become dullness? When does leniency to minority interests become partiality? How is radio to reconcile its own economic interests with public service to the community? As this report deals with public opinion and not with the question of standards, the means of making such an evaluation are not a concern of this book. It is most desirable, however, that an evaluation of program performance be made. From the research standpoint the task is complicated by the transiency of the radio wave. There is as yet little background of experience in keeping records of radio programs or of deciding how such records should be analyzed. Anyone who goes through the existing literature becomes distressed by the divergent ways in which program content is classified. The development of relevant information, and, incidentally, good sampling procedures, is one of the more urgent requirements of radio research.

Yet, knowing what makes a good program, by objective standards, tells only one side of the story. An institution such as radio has social implications which go beyond its immediate product. There is no doubt, for instance, that generally speaking the more money a broadcaster has to build his program structure, the better the technique and talent of the programs. A most impressive program schedule could probably be arranged by taking the top programs of all of the major stations, and developing an "all-star" schedule which could be heard on all radio stations at the same time. But no one would seriously consider such a proposition. The American tradition is to favor divided ownership and regional differentiation.

Other institutions in this country sacrifice top level performance because of ulterior social considerations. Most of our government agencies, for example, are much less efficient than they could be under a dictatorship; but we feel that a certain amount of inefficiency is a small price to pay for our civil liberties and democratic institutions. So, a study of the social structure and social implications of the radio industry would seem to be a second necessary element in an overall evaluation.

One could imagine a radio system which reflects the highest social and aesthetic standards but to which no one would listen. While the radio industry is expected to be a creative leader in the community, nobody wants it to lose contact with what the general public approves of and likes. Approval by public opinion—acceptance by the ultimate consumer—is as important a criterion of evaluation as program standards and social implications.

If the public's reaction to radio is presented and analyzed in much detail in the following pages, it is done with the conviction that a very important piece of information is contributed. But it is also done with the full knowledge that public opinion is only one of several pillars upon which the final evaluation of radio should be based.

Overall Appraisal

Radio is not a single, isolated experience such as seeing a Broadway show, or taking a vacation. It is woven into the daily pattern of our lives year in and year out. A program that appeals to you today may not please you tomorrow. You may like one program and dislike the next. In one phase of a person's life radio may fulfill an important function; in the next phase it may have no place at all. Still, a person may be able to look at it in its entirety and have a general attitude to radio as a whole.

The present survey tackled the problem of overall appraisal by asking each respondent:

> "*In every community, the schools, the newspapers, the local government, each has a different job to do. Around here, would you say that the schools are doing an excellent, good, fair or poor job? How about the newspapers? The radio stations? The local government? The churches?*"

Radio comes out well in this comparison. Table 1 is revealing in several respects. It shows that 82 per cent consider radio's overall service as "excellent" or "good." But the objection could still be made that the four terms used for rating radio are vague and that they may not have the same connotation for all the people interviewed. This is why a comparison is so important. The comparison shows that radio comes off better than any of the four other institutions. Even the churches do not rank as high as radio.

Table 1
OVERALL APPRAISAL OF FIVE INSTITUTIONS[a]

	Radio	Churches	News-papers	Schools	Local government
Excellent	28%	25%	12%	17%	7%
Good	54	51	56	45	38
Fair	10	12	21	18	29
Poor	1	2	4	5	9
Don't know	7	10	7	15	17
Total	100%	100%	100%	100%	100%

[a] When the Minnesota Poll conducted by the *Minneapolis Star Journal* asked this identical question of a cross-section of Minnesotans, in the spring of 1946, it found very similar results. Here are the figures showing how the citizens of Minnesota voted:

	Radio	Churches	Newspapers	Schools	Local government
Excellent	25%	27%	10%	16%	5%
Good	58	52	55	52	49
Fair	12	14	26	18	29
Poor	2	2	5	4	8
No opinion	3	5	4	10	9

It is interesting to reflect for a moment on what this result implies beyond the great overall approval of radio. People seem loth to criticize; with the exception of local government every institution is rated good or better by a majority. The relatively low esteem in which Americans hold their local government is a well-known feature of the American scene.

A question such as the one underlying Table 1 belongs to a group of techniques which are widely used in social research. If one desires to know how an American feels about Turks and Swedes, a common method is to ask whether he would be willing to room with or give his sister in marriage to a member of one of these nationalities. If the question is how much children dislike certain chores, they might be asked whether they would rather eat worms than wash dishes or clean the chicken coop every day. Such attitude questions are never meant to be taken too textually.[2] They give the respondent an opportunity to express in a comparative way how he feels about Swedes or dish washing or radio. Psychological experience has shown that the answers permit the classification of people in broad groups along a line going from a positive to a negative attitude. It is unlikely that many respondents would ever be interested in writing an essay on the kind of a job a radio station or the local government in their community is doing. But from Table 1 it is fairly certain that they feel better about the former than about the latter.

If a general appraisal question of this sort is taken in its proper context, it can be used to bring out a number of interesting details. It turns out, for instance, that the more a person listens the more likely he or she is to say that radio is doing an "excellent job."

Or to put it in a different way: the more radio fits into people's tastes and time schedules, the more will they listen to it. The overall question asking for a general appraisal of radio, therefore, seems to be a useful index of the way people actually behave.

---

2. Gardner Murphy, Lois Murphy and Theodore Newcomb, *Experimental Social Psychology*, New York: Harper and Brothers, 1937, Chapter XIII.

Table 2

PROPORTION WHO APPRAISE RADIO AS "EXCELLENT" ACCORDING TO NUMBER OF HOURS OF EVENING LISTENING

	AMOUNT OF EVENING LISTENING			
	None	2 hours or less	Over 2 to 4 hours	4 or more hours
Radio is doing "excellent" job	14%	26%	32%	41%

A second observation indicates that such a judgment of an institution is influenced by the factor of how willing or able a respondent is to criticize anything. There is a very distinct relationship between what people say about radio and what they say about other institutions. In Table 3 the respondents are classified as to whether they call radio "excellent," "good," or "fair" and "poor." For each of these groups the table lists the proportion that are critical of other institutions (to the extent of calling the job they do only "fair" or "poor"). For example, of the people who rate radio "fair" or "poor," 63 per cent also rate the newspapers "fair" or "poor." Note that the increase in the proportion of critics from left to right in every line of this table is quite marked.

And again the result can be formulated the other way around: the more critical people are of social institutions in general, the more critical will they be of radio.

Annoyances and Dissatisfactions

An overall appraisal such as this may conceal many attitude variations. There is still the possibility that radio may be

Table 3

PROPORTION CRITICAL OF OTHER INSTITUTIONS AMONG PEOPLE WHO HAVE VARIOUS ATTITUDES TOWARD RADIO[a]

Institution judged fair or poor	RADIO JUDGED:		
	Excellent	Good	Fair & Poor
Newspapers	15%	23%	63%
Churches	12	12	31
Schools	17	23	39
Local government	33	37	59

[a] Figures do not add to 100%; each figure shows only the proportion in each group judging other institutions critically.

annoying from time to time, and may leave specific expectations unfulfilled.

At one time or another the majority of people are critical of some phase of radio, just as they are occasionally annoyed by their families or their best loved hobbies. Radio listeners were asked this question:

"*Do you ever feel like criticizing when you listen to the radio?*"

Yes .... 65%   No 35%

It is not quite clear how anyone can say "no" to this general query, since it is a dragnet type of question deliberately designed to bring out all possible criticism, and so it is worth inquiring into what kind of people never feel like criticizing the radio. Table 4 which shows the relation of a critical attitude to amount of radio listening gives a good indication:

Table 4

PROPORTION WHO FEEL ANNOYANCE AT RADIO BY NUMBER OF HOURS EVENING LISTENING

Do you ever feel like criticizing radio?	AMOUNT OF EVENING LISTENING			
	None	2 hours or less	Over 2 to 4 hours	4 or more hours
Yes, feel like criticizing	57%	61%	65%	74%

It might be expected that the people who listen least do so as a result of annoyance with the radio. On the contrary, those people who spend little time listening to the radio are the ones least likely to be irritated. The more people listen, the more likely they are to be annoyed occasionally—to have "lovers quarrels" with radio, so to speak.

So much for minor irritations. How about more serious dissatisfactions? Some people are not satisfied with the amount of local or foreign news they get. The lovers of classical music feel that they do not get enough of what they cherish most. The women who do not like daytime serials feel that there are too many of them on the air. As we shall see, between 20 to 40 per cent, according to the subject, have grievances on a variety of items.

It must be admitted, however, that a direct inquiry into people's dissatisfactions may not yield the most valid results. It is widely recognized in many fields of social research that, psychologically speaking, supply creates demand. The occupation, for instance, which attracts most young people, usually reflects the occupational structure of the community in which they live. The clothes which women like to wear are the clothes they see all around them, in the shop windows and on other women. Within certain limits it is a recognized fact that people like what they get. It is also a fact that nobody knows whether or not a different program fare would be equally, or even more acceptable to average listeners than the present program structure. And few would gainsay that the man in the street lacks the ability to envisage what he would like to hear that is different from what he can listen to now.

Little is known about the degree to which people's tastes are determined by supply. It has been observed that some women who are openly contemptuous of daytime serials get involved in them if some circumstance, such as illness, exposes them to hearing serials for some time. And it is well documented that many songs become popular if they get enough performances on the radio; the whole profession of song-plugging is based on this experience.[3]

On the other hand, serious programs seem to have more acceptance in England than in the United States. But we do not know whether this is due to the larger supply of serious fare on the British system, or to national characteristics of British taste. We may be certain that the classical music supplied by some radio stations creates new music lovers. But here again detailed investigation has shown that such enlargement of musical tastes comes about mainly in social situations where additional pressure is exercised. People who have had some musical education in school or who are acquainted with others who have an interest in music are most likely to be won over by classical music on the radio.[4]

3. Duncan MacDougald, Jr., "The Popular Music Industry," *Radio Research 1941*, by Paul F. Lazarsfeld and Frank N. Stanton, New York: Duell, Sloan and Pearce, 1941, pp. 65-109; and Michael Erdelyi, "The Relation Between 'Radio Plugs' and Sheet Sales of Popular Music," *Journal of Applied Psychology*, XXIV, 6, December, 1940, pp. 696-702.

4. A similar observation, incidentally, has been made in regard to discussion programs. They are more likely to be listened to when some educational organization urges people to listen, organizes listening groups, etc. Paul F. Lazarsfeld, "Audience Building in Educational Broadcasts," *Journal of Educational Sociology*, Vol. XIV, No. 9, May, 1941, pp. 533-542.

In other words, a survey like the present one cannot tell what people would like if they had the opportunity to listen to different radio fare. The desire for more knowledge on this problem is not the idle call for more research; it has eminently practical implications. The request for more serious broadcasts expressed in some quarters is now being countered by other groups with the following argument: all experience shows that the large majority of people do not like to listen to these serious programs; the American system of broadcasting is economically based on advertising revenues, and therefore, the bulk of the radio schedule has to consist of programs which reach large audiences. But suppose that the basic assumptions were not quite so true as we take them to be at the moment. Perhaps, the taste of the listeners could be "elevated" and larger audiences obtained if there was a larger supply of more serious broadcasts with a great deal of promotion put behind them. This would certainly change the situation. There is hardly a broadcaster who, from mere professional pride, would not like to have as valuable a program schedule as possible as long as the economic foundation of his business did not suffer. Many of them would enjoy being trail blazers if they could believe that in the end a larger group of listeners would follow their lead. This is the reason why it would be so important to know more about the speed with which and the conditions under which the habits of the listeners could be elevated to what is commonly referred to as a higher level.

Turning now to details, it can be assumed that foremost in many readers' minds is the question, "What about advertising?"

Chapter II.   ADVERTISING

ANYONE WHO HAS EVER PARTICIPATED IN a discussion of the American system of broadcasting will have noticed how soon the topic leads to the subject of advertising. And he will also remember the ultimate futility of the debate. The participants in this kind of discussion usually do not like to listen to commercials. But what can be said in the face of the fact that radio has to be financed in some way? It is possible to charge people for their newspapers, but it is impracticable to make a person pay for an individual act of listening.

Twenty-five years ago the idea prevailed that the manufacturers of radio sets would carry the expenses of broadcasting in order to stimulate their sales. But this solution would have been possible only if the technical expenses of broadcasting had remained relatively moderate. In the course of radio's early development, some station owners started to pay and to compete for talent, which greatly increased broadcasting expenses. At the same time, it became clear that once the country was saturated with receiving sets, the sale of replacements could never finance broadcasting indefinitely. It became obvious that a more general system of financing was essential.

The commercial support of radio crept up almost inadverently in the first phase of broadcasting. Many early stations were started by people who wanted to advertise their own services. A few stations began taking fees for advertising someone else's product. Thus the idea of radio as an advertising medium was born.[1]

---

1. For accounts of the history of broadcasting see: Thomas Porter Robinson, *Radio Networks and the Federal Government*, New York: Columbia University Press, 1943; and Gleason L. Archer, *Big Business and Radio*, New York: American Historical Company, 1939.

It would be tempting to say that there was a point at which two solutions offered themselves; one to levy a tax on every set owner, just as much of our road building is financed by a gasoline tax paid by the people who use the road; the other, commercial sponsorship of radio programs. Actually there was never a serious decision made between tax support and the commercial support which advertising might offer. The economic mood of the early 20's was too much opposed to any government participation in economic matters. The present system of commercial radio is an outgrowth of the economic philosophy of the time.

Today, advertising and radio are intimately linked in everyone's mind, though the manner in which the American citizen pays for his radio is not so different from the way he pays for his newspapers and magazines. Notwithstanding the few cents he pays for his printed media, the real costs of both are paid for indirectly. Regardless of whether unit costs of production are lowered by sales, stimulated by advertising, whenever he buys a national brand of merchandise, to some extent he also pays for the story he reads or the program he listens to in his leisure time.

There is, however, an important difference in the way the customer is made aware of this intricate system of financing. He is not compelled to look at advertisements in the printed media if he does not choose, but it is more difficult for him to avoid hearing the radio commercial. As a result, radio advertising has been a continuous topic of conversation since the inception of sponsored broadcasts.

Strangely enough, in spite of the great interest in the topic, little research has been done that gives any clearcut evidence as to how the population as a whole feels about radio commercials. A review of what has been published on this subject in magazines and newspapers could be made but it would probably reveal a rather one-sided picture. It might be no more reliable than if public feeling on the last two presidential elections had been forecast by a survey of newspaper opinion. Such a study would have shown that 85 per cent of the newspapers disapproved of the late President Roosevelt. And yet, it is a matter of public record that this finding would not have reflected the true feeling of the country. It is believed that this present study is the first one to record direct and comprehensive information on the public's attitude toward radio advertising.

The Description of an Attitude

To describe the results of any survey on people's attitudes is not altogether a simple straightforward matter. In studying an election, people can be asked whether they will or will not vote for a candidate. But voting figures do not really describe the full complex of attitudes. Some people do indeed vote for a man because they approve of him, but other votes may mean that the candidate, although bad, is not as bad as his opponent. Sometimes people vote *against* one candidate rather than *for* the other. And some people vote for a man whose name they hardly know, let alone his record, just because a friend or a relative has asked them to do so. But to reveal the full range of attitudes toward a man or a topic, the inquiry must be approached in a variety of ways. The following paragraphs indicate many of the considerations involved in any effort to give a reliable picture of how people feel about a topic under investigation.

The first task is to determine whether the topic in question is in people's minds before they have any reason to suspect the subject of the research. In the present survey the following question exemplifies this approach:

"*Do you ever feel like criticizing when you listen to the radio?*"

Two-thirds answered "yes" and were then asked: "What are some of your main criticisms?" The proportion of the critics who did and who did not mention advertising as one of their annoyances are shown in Table 5.

Table 5

PROPORTION EVER ANNOYED AT RADIO[a]

	Per cent
Ever annoyed: At advertising	29%
Not at advertising	35
Never annoyed	36
Total	100%

[a] For details see Appendix B, Question 17.

It appears that radio advertising comes to the minds of about a third of the people automatically when the inquiry touches on the general criticism of broadcasting. But this is, so to speak, the one extreme of the situation. It represents only those people who are so concerned about radio commercials that it is one of the first criticisms they volunteer. The same problem may be approached from the other extreme, by specifically suggesting to people that there may be something undesirable in radio advertising and then seeing how they react. The following question was asked for this purpose:

"*If your radio programs could be produced without advertising, would you prefer it that way?*"

Interestingly enough, both approaches bring about the same result. Around one-third of the listeners think of advertising as an annoyance on their own initiative, and about the same proportion state, upon direct suggestion, that radio without advertising would be preferable.

Table 6

PROPORTION WHO PREFER RADIO WITH OR WITHOUT ADVERTISING

Would prefer programs produced:	Per cent
With advertising	62%
Without advertising	35
No opinion	3
Total	100%

But this inquiry is not yet at an end. The situation may not be this simple. It may be doing violence to people's true feelings to force their answers into a "yes-no" mold. They should perhaps be given an opportunity to choose among more refined possibilities. A question was therefore devised which permitted each respondent to state his attitude on a continuum ranging from unqualified approval to complete disapproval. Table 7 shows the wording of this question and at the same time gives the distribution of answers.

Again it is found that a third of the people (26% and 7%) have a really negative feeling toward commercials.[2] This corroborates the previous findings and places them on safer ground. Probing for attitudes toward radio commercials in three different ways seems to confirm the fact that about a third of the radio listening public is anti-advertising.

This consistency of findings has an important psychological implication. It indicates that the topic of radio commercials is one on which many people have already reflected. A very direct question does not add much to their voluntary associations; a more complex question does not lead to very different

[2]. See pages 19 and 20 for evidence of the genuine differences in attitude expressed in Table 7.

results from a simple one. People's attitudes toward radio commercials are, as a psychologist would call it, fairly "well structured."

Table 7

A MORE DETAILED QUESTION
ON ATTITUDE TO RADIO ADVERTISING

"Which one of these four statements comes closest to what you yourself think about advertising on the radio?" — Per cent

"I'm *in favor* of advertising on the radio because it tells me about the things I want to buy"	23%
"*I don't particularly mind* advertising on the radio. It doesn't interfere too much with my enjoyment of the program"	41
"I don't like advertising on the radio but *I'll put up with it*"	26
"I think all advertising should be *taken off* the radio"	7
No opinion	3
Total	100%

But confirming the result in three different questions is still not the final answer unless it can be shown that it is the *same* third who always object to advertising on each different question. While it is reassuring to get the same results in three different approaches, there is still the danger that people's answers may be perfunctory and inconsistent. If they were pro-advertising on one question and against advertising on another, it would be only a chance result that the findings always show opposition from about one third. The way to test this possibility is to see whether people answer different questions in the same way. As one example of these correlations, Table 8 shows the relationship between the general attitude question and the question on whether the respondents would prefer their radio programs without advertising (other examples supporting the same conclusion appear in the Appendix[3]). These results seem to dissipate the last shadow of doubt concerning the reliability of the estimate that about a third are opponents of radio advertising.

Table 8

PROPORTION WHO PREFER RADIO WITH OR WITHOUT ADVERTISING ACCORDING TO GENERAL ATTITUDE TOWARD ADVERTISING

	ATTITUDE TOWARD ADVERTISING			
Would you prefer radio without advertising?	In favor	Don't mind	Put up with	Take off air
Yes	4%	20%	73%	96%
No	96	80	27	4
Total	100%	100%	100%	100%

The table shows high consistency in two respects. First, practically all the people who like advertising very much and those who are very much opposed to it stick to their guns however they are questioned. Ninety-six per cent who indicate a favorable attitude toward advertising on one question also say that they prefer their programs with advertising on the other question. Ninety-six per cent who say that they think advertising should be abolished want radio without advertising on the other question. Second, the difference between the second and third columns is also marked. If people "don't

3. Appendix D, Tables 1A and 1B.

mind" advertising, 80 per cent of them are willing to take their programs as they get them now. But if people who merely "put up with" commercials had a choice, 73 per cent of them would prefer programs without commercials.

This table then, and similar ones reported in the Appendix,[4] not only corroborate the fact that the people have structured opinions and language habits regarding commercials, but they also establish the fact that those people who make a distinction between "not minding" and "just putting up with" advertising are making a real distinction.

Why Should Anyone Like Commercials?

In many ways this result is very surprising. It is safe to say that the finding that only a third of the radio listening public is anti-advertising contradicts the predictions of many casual observers. Haven't we all had people tell us in no uncertain terms how terrible radio commercials are? Wouldn't we have laid high odds that at least three-fourths of all radio listeners felt strongly on the subject? The situation is somewhat reminiscent of the Park Avenue lady, who claimed the last presidential election was a fraud because for weeks she had met no one who did not intend to vote for the Republican candidate.

And yet, why should people be in favor of advertising? Mere statistics do not supply the full answer to this question. It is also necessary to understand some of the psychological implications behind the fact that the survey did not reveal greater numbers of complaints against commercials. There is good reason for people to resist any attempt to try to sell them something. A second glance at Table 7 gives a clue to an interpretation of the findings. While two-thirds of the people in this country are not opposed to advertising, only 23 per cent actually come out for it positively and affirmatively. But some of these, in various parts of the interview, made comments which elucidate vividly the reasons for their approval:

4. Appendix D, Tables 1A and 1B.

"Radio has improved. I get quite a bit of information from the advertisements."
(Mother of Navy engineer, Tacoma, Wash.)
"I think advertising is the progress of our country."
(Insurance and real estate broker, Adams, Mass.)
"Home people out in the country need the radio advertising."
(Wife of janitor, Prineville, Ore.)
"I might fuss about ads on the radio but truthfully I would be lost without them."
(Wife of manufacturer, Miami, Fla.)
"I think all the soap ads are good. I used to buy a different kind every day when I could get it."
(Farmer's wife, Morganfield, Ky.)

A variety of elements probably coalesce in this attitude. Remember that there are many people who find real human enjoyment in sitting by the window, watching passers-by in the street; many who read the weekly local newspaper to find out all they can about the other people in town; many who go window-shopping just to know what other people can afford to buy. Similarly, for some people perhaps radio commercials are a part of the great human interest story of which they never tire.[5]

To this group should be added others who find advertising constructively useful. Some people feel that they learn something from advertisements. There is circumstantial evidence on this point from a question which will be introduced in more detail in a later chapter, a question about what people learn from the radio. For the present purpose only those people who say they get practical information from the radio, such as home-making or farm talks, are selected for examination. Table 9 classifies people according to their attitudes toward advertising. For each of the resulting four groups is shown the proportion who have acquired some practical information from the radio.

[5]. For the reliance of urban readers on the newspapers for human interest, see Helen MacGill Hughes, *News and the Human Interest Story*, Chicago: University of Chicago Press, 1940.

Table 9

RELATIONSHIP BETWEEN LEARNING INFORMATION OF PRACTICAL VALUE FROM THE RADIO AND GENERAL ATTITUDE TOWARD ADVERTISING[a]

General attitude toward advertising	Per cent learning practical information from radio
In favor of advertising; it tells me about things I want to buy	43%
Don't particularly mind advertising; doesn't interfere too much	30
Don't like advertising; but will put up with it	26
All advertising should be taken off the radio	17

[a] Appendix D, Table 2.

The people who take a favorable stand toward commercials are also those who report most frequently that radio gives them useful hints for their practical problems in everyday life. This close correlation does not prove but does suggest that some of the practical informative value of radio lies in the advertising.

There is still a third factor which should be considered. The public has become accustomed to expecting sponsored programs to be more glamorous or technically better than sustaining programs. It is commonly accepted in the trade that the same program, when it acquires a sponsor, finds a larger audience. It is quite possible that some of the people are afraid that without the added endowments which advertising bestows, programs would be less entertaining than they are now.

There seem, then, to be three main considerations which make for positive approval of commercial advertising—its human interest value, its usefulness, and the fact that in general the most popular programs are sponsored.

How about those people who do not really like advertising but still do not feel sufficiently strongly about it to demand that it be radically changed or removed? Not much interpretation is possible here. To a large extent they are probably people of rather even temperament and uncritical minds. They enjoy radio and are not too disturbed about what goes with it. Still, a number of them indicate that they have given thought to the matter. Some of them imply that listening to advertising is one of their contributions to the existence of radio. They may say nothing scathing about advertising, but concentrate more on the high quality of programming under commercial sponsorship.

> "Someone has to pay so that we can get the good programs. We wouldn't get the programs we get if it weren't paid for by sponsors, you can rest assured of that." (Machinist, Worcester, Mass.)
> "If advertising were taken off, our programs would not be as good and would to a certain extent lack interest." (Wife of engineer, Glendale, Cal.)

But others who are just as aware of this link between advertising and their radio programs do not make such tolerant statements:

> "I like the programs enough so I'll stand the advertising." (Owner of electrical shop, Helena, Mont.)
> "It would make it more interesting if you didn't have to listen to the advertising but, of course, advertising has to be." (Wife of linotypist, Portland, Ore.)
> "The commercials are a nuisance. They interrupt the programs and they talk too much. But I guess we have to stand

it as we get the service for nothing." (Retired police sergeant, Belleville, N. J.)

The attitudes expressed in these last comments are not as pleasant as those quoted in the first group. In spite of their acceptance of advertising, their air of resignation is enough to give pause to public spirited and responsible broadcasters. Their comments indicate the desirability of reconsidering the treatment of radio advertising from a fresh point of view.

Danger Signals

It would be a great temptation to stop with the well substantiated finding that two-thirds of the population either like or do not mind advertising on the air. It is a result which would certainly dispel many suspicions to the contrary long rampant among critics most of whom have given the matter only superficial attention.

But suppose there had not been so much controversy about whether people do or do not actively dislike commercials,—would the results then be equally reassuring? Advertising is a vital element in the texture of American broadcasting—but only 23 per cent really like it, while a third exhibit varying degrees of opposition to it. While the situation is much better than most people would have thought, it is certainly not without serious implications for the radio industry.

A variety of specific danger signals can be added to such general considerations. There is, for instance, the fact that 35 per cent of the people would prefer to have radio programs produced without advertising, while only 10 per cent feel the same way about newspapers.[6] As most radio listeners are also newspaper readers, this provides a continuous incentive to invidious comparisons.

Again, there is the fact that the opponents of advertising feel so very strongly and are so articulate in promulgating their opinions. On the other hand, the defenders of commer-

6. Appendix B, Question 20.

cials make mild friendly statements when questioned directly and it is doubtful whether it would occur to them to volunteer such remarks. Here, for example, are some comments which illustrate the violence of the attacks of some of the opponents: "Most annoying", "Hated by millions", "It's a lot of hokum", "The whole thing is ridiculous", "They say it over and over and it's very tiresome", "I can't stand it", "It makes you disgusted with the product."

But the main danger signal is yet to be mentioned. While incidental annoyances and even some specific dissatisfactions do not seem to affect people's general appraisal of radio appreciably, attitudes toward advertising color what people feel about radio as a whole.[7] The more irritated people are toward commercials the less likely they are to react favorably to radio as a whole. This may be seen in the following analysis:

Table 10

PROPORTION THINKING RADIO IS DOING "EXCELLENT" JOB IN COMMUNITY ACCORDING TO GENERAL ATTITUDE TO ADVERTISING[a]

General attitude toward advertising	Proportion thinking radio doing an excellent job
In favor of advertising; it tells me about things I want to buy	39%
Don't particularly mind advertising; doesn't interfere too much	29
Don't like advertising; but will put up with it	25
All advertising should be taken off the radio	24

[a] Appendix D, Table 2.

7. Appendix D, Table 3.

Notice the decline of favorable opinion toward radio in each successive group, indicating how attitudes toward advertising and an overall judgment of radio tend to go together. From a practical point of view, this means that one point at which broadcasters can perhaps increase their public approval to some extent lies in the way they handle commercials. Before discussing in detail how this could be done, however, it is obviously necessary to examine more closely what most arouses the opposition of the critical minority.

What's Wrong with Commercials

A careful analysis of all available anti-advertising comments leads to the conclusion that the following factors, separately or in combinations, are the main features about commercials that bother people.[8]

(a) *Volume and Position.* The mere existence of commercials can become bothersome. Complaints on this score divide into three groups: that there are too many of them, that they are too long, and that they interrupt the program.

Some of these objections, of course, are naive. Some listeners fail to wonder who pays the piper but merely feel that the station is stealing "their time" for the commercial messages.

> "When I listen to the radio I expect only to enjoy the program." (Teacher, Adams, Mass.)
> "We can get all of the advertising in newspapers and magazines. I prefer to listen only to be entertained." (Grocery clerk, Hanson, Ky.)

Other people are more realistic and object only when commercials are too frequent and follow one another too closely, or they object to their length.

The interruption of the listening mood by the middle commercial comes in for bitter comment. One respondent remarks about a commentator:

8. Appendix B, Questions 17 to 26.

"He makes me so mad. He gets me so interested and then switches to the product. He's a good guy but when he interrupts with the commercial, he is terrible." (School teacher, New Iberia, La.)

On the other hand, people frequently praise commercials when they are well integrated with the program. When they are asked to give examples of good programs, many of the comments are like the following:

"Fibber McGee and Molly. He works it in with the story. Doesn't just stop program and put in commercial. It goes with the story." (Office boy, Brooklyn, N. Y.)
"March of Time. They bring it in so naturally without slapping you in the face." (Vice-president of construction company, Clayton, Mo.)

The number, length and position of commercials are not, therefore, an absolute shortcoming. People do not consider advertising an interruption if it is skillfully inserted. They also mind the length of the commercial less if the content is interesting. As a matter of fact, it is a common psychological experience that a dull ad may appear longer than an interesting one even if the two messages are actually of the same length. This makes the next group of objections especially noteworthy.

(b) *Uninteresting Content*. People mind commercials less if they contain interesting information or a good joke. But if they are just an accumulation of words strung together from the manufacturer's point of view, they create a feeling of monotony and repetitiousness which is especially repugnant to many listeners. Many are inclined to make remarks such as these:

"They don't tell you anything about the product. I am bored with them." (Milk man, Wethersfield, Conn.)
"They use about five minutes and harp and harp until you

think you will go crazy and can't even remember what they say." (Shoemaker, Milwaukee, Ore.)
"The fellow who talks about it is very dull. No life in him." (Barber, Brooklyn, N. Y.)

On the other hand, people are appreciative if the commercials either entertain them or give them some real information.

"About bananas. Don't put bananas in the refrigerator. It comes all day long over all stations. Educational advertising tells about how to handle bananas." (Teacher, Glencoe, Mo.)
"Light Crust Flour, Magic Miller Flour. Tell how you can use the sacks and how good the flour is." (Farmer's wife, Sheridan, Ark.)

There is considerable relationship between the criticism of length of commercials and the present one, interest. One respondent says he especially dislikes commercials on soap powders because:

"They take too much time—6 out of 15 minutes of advertising." (Chain store manager, Philadelphia, Pa.)

Certainly no soap program devotes 40 per cent of its time to its commercial, but if uninteresting, plugs may easily seem that long.

(c) *Overselling*. In the advertising trade this is what is called "hard selling". Strong superlatives, insistent voices which overemphasize the plea to buy, detailed accumulations of advantages and similar devices get on many people's nerves.

People complain in different ways that advertising claims too much:

"They try to make you think you'll be a robust man if you smoke a certain cigarette." (Painting contractor, Escondido, Cal.)
"They claim too much for their product and it is so silly to think that by using their products is the only way for a

woman to get a man." (Wife of proprietor, variety store, Worcester, Mass.)

"I don't like any ad that suggests something bad will happen if you don't use it." (Sales engineer of steam control equipment, Belleville, N. J.)

"Soap advertisements. I fail to ever find it as good as they say it is. They're good but not that good." (Widow living on savings, Escondido, Cal.)

On the other hand, people feel relieved if a program doesn't contain "hard selling" commercials:

"Bell Telephone and the DuPont programs. There is no high pressure advertising in it. They are higher class programs." (Student, Pittsfield, Mass.)

"The Ford Hour. Because it's adult—they use good taste—they don't push it." (Salesman, Paterson, N. J.)

(d) *Violation of Taboos.* Depending on the way people have been brought up, different things offend their sense of propriety. When someone mentions one of them, they call it "bad taste." Some people censure medical advertisements which bring up topics which are usually excluded from their general conversation. Many people feel that it is "bad taste" to link personal success with such external devices as wearing apparel and cosmetics. Some dislike it if soups are termed glorious, or if people are urged to forget the troubles of our times by turning to another brand of coffee. Others object to certain products being advertised at all. Outstanding in this classification is the opposition to the advertisement of alcoholic beverages.

It is difficult to keep track of all these taboos which radio is supposed to avoid, because they vary so greatly from one social group to another, and in terms of different sections of the country. The present survey submitted a list of products to people and asked:

"Are there any products listed here which you think should not be advertised over the radio?"

Half the radio listeners did not object to any of the products on the list. The proportion who disapproved of each product is reproduced in Table 11.

Table 11

PROPORTION OPPOSED TO ADVERTISING OF DIFFERENT PRODUCTS ON THE RADIO

Product opposed	Per cent[a]
Whiskey	42%
Beer	36
Liver remedies	22
Laxatives	20
Headache remedies	16
Cigarettes	12
Deodorants	11
Gasoline	5
Tooth paste	5
Bread	4
Ice cream	4
Automobiles	4
All should be allowed to advertise	49%

[a] Percentages add to more than 100% because more than one answer per person was possible.

These overall percentages conceal rather wide group differences.[9] The objection to whiskey advertising is chiefly a moral one. It occurs most frequently in smaller towns and more among women than among men. On the other hand, the objection to laxatives, deodorants, and so on is a more aesthetic one. It occurs more frequently among highly educated people

9. Appendix D, Table 4.

and especially among those who in the course of the interview reveal relatively great sophistication on other questions.[10]

(e) *Attention-getting Devices.* Listeners frequently consider "silly," advertising which is in the form of jingles, singing commercials, dramatized skits, or which includes attention-getting sound effects. Some say that such devices offend their intelligence. It is not easy to understand the psychological element behind this objection, especially since other listeners find in them relief from the monotony of more stereotyped commercials. It is certainly difficult to develop a consistent policy if listeners' reactions are as contradictory as the following pairs of quotations illustrate:

"Them singing ditties. They just kinda make you happy." (Wife of laborer, Texarkana, Tex.)

"Singing commercials are so silly—about the mentality of a six-year-old." (Wife of engineer, Tacoma, Wash.)

"Ivory Soap. Like to sing the song. Children enjoy it." (Wife of elevator operator, Bronx, N. Y.)

"The singing, the jingles—the whole thing is ridiculous." (Wife of welder, Belleville, N. J.)

It might be possible that attitudes toward attention-getting devices vary with type of program; that perhaps some sound effects might be especially offensive in connection with a serious musical or news program, but not when the context is more appropriate.

A tie-in probably also exists between attention-getting devices and people's dislike of repetition. When the same jingles are repeated day after day, week after week and month after month at the same hour and the same minute, an initial pleasure may well turn into an ultimate surfeit.

10. The first two figures of Table 11 are interesting from another point of view. Most radio stations accept beer, but reject whiskey advertisements. This is obviously not due to the 6 per cent difference in public reaction, but to a variety of general considerations. This again points to the fact that public opinion data are only one of the factors which enter into the appraisal of a social institution.

What Should Be Done About Commercials

For a rough orientation, then, it may be said that people who dislike commercials are bothered by five major groups of factors:

(1) Commercials are too long, too frequent and interruptive;
(2) They are boring and uninteresting;
(3) They make unwarranted claims and make them in too intensive a form;
(4) They sometimes violate a variety of social taboos;
(5) They use attention-getting devices which are unpleasant to some people.

These five psychological factors are certainly not independent of each other and they frequently occur simultaneously. Yet, they are sufficiently distinctive so that it is possible to discuss what could be done to remedy each one of them.

With regard to the first point, nothing would be easier than to shorten commercials and tone down their claims. Why isn't it being done?

The answer is simple. If one advertiser does it and the other does not, the first would be afraid that the second would sell more goods. Actually there is no published evidence that longer and harder selling commercials are necessarily more successful selling devices. But the competitive situation is likely to keep many individual advertisers from making drastic reductions. One way to pave the way for improvement and to protect advertisers would be for the industry as a whole to take action. The National Association of Broadcasters asks its members to agree not to use more than a limited amount of program time for their commercials. It is hard to say whether or not a further reduction in length of commercials would be feasible at the moment. But there is little doubt that the

NAB would be well advised to keep an ever vigilant eye open to make certain that the stated time is not exceeded by individual stations to the detriment of the entire industry.

The "middle commercial," incidentally, offers a special problem. It interrupts the program and is, therefore, a frequent object of resentment. At the same time, it is one of the surest ways to reach the listeners with a sales message. Thus, it might eventually become a symbol in the struggle between balancing commercial advantages and maintaining the good will of the audience.

It is easier to measure time than to measure claims. But in judging overselling there are certain obvious criteria on which to work: superlative descriptions, urgent admonitions to buy at once, implications as to the dire results of not buying a product. It would undoubtedly be a wise idea if a representative sample of commercials were to be studied for such elements. Tests could be made with listeners to spot the kind of wording and delivery which is likely to create antagonism. In the end the NAB might promulgate certain "do's" and don'ts."

There is obviously one special difficulty in this whole picture. If all advertisers and all radio stations were to agree on shorter and less hard selling commercials, no one would be handicapped competitively. But radio as a whole might still be at a disadvantage in competing with the printed media and other advertising devices. While no evidence exists to show that this would actually be the case, the industry might eventually be forced to accept some additional restriction because of the special position of social responsibility it occupies as licensee of a public franchise.

The fact that critics find commercials uninteresting and boring raises a different question. It is perfectly possible to write more interesting commercials, and it has been shown how appreciative many listeners are with the more clever productions. Here radio writers are in the same situation as any other producer. Just as automobiles and motion pictures have improved technically from year to year, so it is to be expected that the skill of writing more engaging commercials will continue to develop. Self-regulation and admonitions are likely to speed up this process. Perhaps it is important that the public's appreciation for more interesting commercials be brought repeatedly to the attention of copywriters and advertising agencies. How clever they will be in developing the appropriate techniques is simply a matter of time.

Attention-getting devices such as jingles, sound effects and dramatizations present an even more complicated problem. While there are many critics, a great number of people consider them more acceptable than some other types of commercials. It is probable, however, that these advertising novelties achieve much of their unpopularity from their continual repetition. If this is the case, a partial solution would be to combat surfeit with more frequent changes and more original ideas.

This leaves the violation of taboos to be discussed, and, at this point, the question arises whether there is any feasible solution. Taboos are relative. A few decades ago a cigarette smoking woman was an outrage. Today she is a familiar feature of the American scene. And as far as remedies for upset stomachs go, an actual study of the commercials will probably show that radio stations exercise great care in the language they condone.[11] Study of a variety of aspects of radio, such as the

11. CBS will permit no broadcasting for any product which describes graphically or repellently any internal bodily functions, symptomatic results of internal disturbances, or matters which are generally not considered acceptable topics in social groups. This policy will specifically exclude: all advertising of laxatives as such, and the advertising of any laxative properties in any other product; depilatories; deodorants; other broadcasting which, by its nature, presents questions of good taste in connection with radio listening. *New Policies, A Statement to the Public, to Advertisers, and to Advertising Agencies,* The Columbia Broadcasting System, May 15, 1935, pp. 7-9.

NBC's classifications of products and services which are unacceptable for commercial broadcast over the facilities of the National Broadcasting Company follow: professional services; stocks and bonds; cures; cathartics; hygiene products; deodorants; reducing agents; restoratives; fortune telling;

content of daytime serials or the lyrics of popular songs, has shown that this new medium is extremely sensitive to the mores of the community. As a matter of fact, the opinion has even been voiced that radio is too sensitive and that it would be more progressive if it offended someone once in a while. On the whole, however, the respecting of taboos can safely be left to the broadcasters themselves. They are probably so well representative of the American public that they share its repressions and anxieties in just the right proportions.

This brief speculation on the major shortcomings of commercials leads to the conclusion that the two complaints on which the industry could most profitably work at the moment are length and frequency of commercials, on the one hand, and the aggressiveness of the sales message, on the other. This conclusion is corroborated by a research finding of the present survey.

A question was included in the inquiry which was meant to provide another measure of people's feeling about commercials. Each respondent was given a list of ten criticisms of advertising and asked: "Would you tell me which ones, if any, you feel strongly about?"

Table 12 lists the objections in the order in which they were shown the respondent and shows the proportion of people who feel strongly that each of the criticisms is justified.

This statistical material sheds some light on the importance of the five groups of factors which have already been singled out as the main objections to commercials.

The complaint against the *volume and position* of commercials comes up in these three items: 35 per cent say that commercials interrupt programs, 30 per cent say they are too long,

---

mortuaries, etc. (cemeteries, casket manufacturers); wines and liquors (beer acceptable subject to local and federal laws); firearms and fireworks; matrimonial agencies; racing organizations; employment services; schools. *NBC Program Policies and Working Manual*, National Broadcasting Company, Inc., 1945, Part III, pp. 18-19.

26 per cent say that there are too many of them. The objection that commercials spoil the fun of listening is the most frequent one in this group; it also seems that a somewhat higher proportion of people mind length rather than frequency of ads.

Table 12
CRITICISMS OF RADIO ADVERTISING

Criticism	Per cent*
Too long	30%
Bad taste	13
Too detailed	13
Too much singing	15
Too repetitious	32
Interrupt programs	35
Silly	31
Too many jingles	18
Claim too much for product	33
Too many of them	26
Don't object strongly to any	27

*Percentages add to more than 100% because more than one answer per person was possible.

It is not easy to distinguish *dullness of content* from "too long" as an objection. Yet, it is probably safe to say that two of the ten classifications refer to the second factor of the preceding analysis, to wit: monotony. Thirty-two per cent say that commercials are too repetitious and 13 per cent say that they are too detailed. The marked difference between those two figures gives an important hint. People apparently do not mind details so much if they are fairly noteworthy; they are much more concerned about being bored.

One item in the list checked by 33 per cent reads explicitly: "Commercials *claim too much* for the product." In a way then, it may be said that the three objections of time-consuming, monotony and overselling are mentioned equally often.

Bad taste is mentioned by only 13 per cent. This is the only one of the five areas of objections which is mentioned considerably less frequently than the others. This seems to bring out the special care which broadcasters exercise on this point and which was mentioned before (page 34).

Another factor which at first sight seems of lesser importance is the *attention-getting* devices. Only 18 per cent of the respondents checked "too many jingles," and 15 per cent "too much singing." It is likely, however, that these percentages do not tell the whole story. Thirty-one per cent of all respondents said they disliked "silly" commercials. Probably many of these comments refer to attention-getting devices.

It may be concluded, therefore, that four of the factors—quantity, dullness, overselling, and attention-getting devices are of approximately equal importance.[12]

But enough of advertising. Commercials are after all not the center of the radio world. Most of radio's time and most of the listener's interest are given to the programs themselves, and there are problems aplenty in programming. So the discussion now turns to the different ways in which listeners use radio, to the various functions which radio has for them.

12. For a further analysis on this point see Appendix D, Tables 5, 6 and 7.

Chapter III.   RADIO FOR WHAT?

The Broadcasters' Dilemma

THERE are some elements in people's attitudes toward radio which a simple survey can hardly catch. It is easy to distinguish one newspaper from another by its name, the look of its banner head, and even by its type and format. But for many listeners the loud speaker tends to make radio one continuous accoustical experience. A reader can scan the contents of a current issue of a magazine, and then pick out what he wants to read; very few people have a clear picture of what is to be found in a station's weekly program log. Comic strips can be compared by looking at one beside the other; but the listener to one radio program cannot possibly compare it with others on the air at the same time.

In a way this makes for unintelligent listening in the sense that people do not frequently size up the available supply of programs and then choose that which is most appropriate to their individual tastes and purposes.[1] The program logs published in the daily press are of some help. But lists of titles strung together in small type are not conducive to discriminating choice. To be sure, it would be difficult to scan all the new books which appear in the course of a week. But a whole profession of book critics review and digest what is available. By comparison the field of radio criticism is in its infancy.[2] In recent years, the broadcasters themselves have begun to cross-announce programs which are to come later on the same sta-

---

[1]. Henry Morgan blames the scarcity of good programs on the fact that many high class programs have been taken off the air for lack of audience. See: "What's Wrong with Radio? 'The Audience'," *New York Times Magazine*, April 21, 1946, p. 12.

[2]. Robert J. Landry, "Wanted: Radio Critics," *Public Opinion Quarterly*, December, 1940, pp. 620-629, and *Who, What, Why is Radio?*, New York: G. W. Stewart, 1942, Ch. 9; and Charles Siepmann, "Further Thoughts on Radio Criticism," *Public Opinion Quarterly*, June, 1941, pp. 308-312.

tion. But the problem of letting the radio audience know what is available still remains largely unsolved.[3]

If it is true that the public knows very little of what to expect in forthcoming broadcasts, it is also true that only in rather general terms does the broadcaster know what kinds of people like to listen to different types of programs. Slowly the radio industry has become aware of how widely varied is the composition of listeners for different programs. And how helpful is such knowledge? The general nature of the word "broadcasting" itself intimates that the more specific the listeners' taste the greater the headaches for the industry. One station can satisfy only one type of listening desire at a time. Should stations try to give certain hours to certain types of listeners? Should there be an understanding between different stations to provide a variety of program types at the same time? What then becomes of free competition? What about minority tastes—how can their cases be arbitrated?

This is not the place to answer all these questions; but no discussion of any aspect of radio is possible without injecting some information on the complexity of this problem of programming. The present survey contained the question:

> "Here's a set of cards listing different kinds of radio programs. Would you mind looking through those cards, and telling me the types of programs you like to listen to in the daytime?"
> "Now which types of programs there do you like to listen to in the evening?"

The nature of the information obtained from asking people what they like to listen to can best be brought out by a comparison with the well-known program ratings. A rating tells with more or less precision how many people listen to a given program at a given time. Such actual listening figures are only limited indices of people's radio preferences. If two equally

---

3. Douglas D. Connah, *How to Build the Radio Audience*, New York: Harpers, 1938; and Paul F. Lazarsfeld, *Radio and the Printed Page*, New York: Duell, Sloan and Pearce, 1940, pp. 121-132.

fine programs are on the air at the same time, each will obviously get only half the rating that the same program would get if it happened to have no competition. The same program broadcast at 8 o'clock in the evening is likely to get several times the audience that it would get at 3 o'clock in the afternoon. If there are many of a certain type of program on the air it is unfair to compare audience ratings with a type which is broadcast only infrequently. Competition, time on the air, and extent of supply are then, at least, three factors which tend to limit the value of audience ratings alone insofar as they reveal people's attitudes toward radio programs. To this it must be added that ratings, usually obtained over the telephone, ordinarily yield nothing beyond the total size of the audience, generally tell nothing about its composition—whether the bulk of the listeners are young or old people, educated or uneducated.

The questions on listeners' general program preferences just quoted do much to cut through these difficulties. But their use requires caution in another direction. Whether a person did or did not listen to a certain program can be established with a fair amount of accuracy. Whether he "likes to listen" to a certain type of program is a much looser question. At the one extreme it can mean that the listener is enthusiastic about it, or at the other extreme that he listens to it only because there is nothing more desirable available at that time.

Furthermore, there is no clearly established terminology for program types. Therefore, such answers are somewhat dependent upon the way the question is worded. The reader will find some interesting examples in the Appendix.[4] If asked about "radio plays," some listeners will think of daytime serials, even if they are asked afterward specifically about the latter type. If questioned about "radio plays completed in one program," the figures are somewhat changed.

Still this type of general preference question yields valuable

4. Appendix D, Tables 8 and 9.

information—especially if attention is focussed, as it is here, on the variety of tastes among different listener groups. Two precautions help to increase confidence in the results to be summarized. One is that conclusions are drawn only on rather large numerical differences. Secondly, the results are corroborated by many other studies. For every point made in this chapter, other studies made under different circumstances can be adduced and with somewhat varying questions which have brought to light similar findings.[5]

New Programs

The questions quoted above are therefore used as a general guide to what "radio" means to different people in terms of the programs to which they are most likely to listen. Seventy-one per cent say they like to listen to news in the daytime; 76 per cent in the evening. South and West, men and women, village and metropolis, only slight variations are found. In all groups seven or eight out of ten people say they like to listen to news programs either day or evening.[6] Only one other program type (comedy and variety, as will be seen later) has an equally general appeal.

The function of radio as a purveyor of news has steadily grown in importance, partly because world events have made the American people much more news conscious. About 15 or 20 years ago, it seemed for a time that newspapers and radio stations might engage in a bitter struggle to be the nation's main source of news. Today it has become apparent that they each play their own role. When people are asked, "Which one gives you the most complete news?", 67 per cent give the bow to newspapers. When asked, "Which one gives you the latest news most quickly?", 94 per cent give credit to radio.[7]

5. F. L. Whan, *The Kansas Radio Audience of 1945*, Wichita, Kan.: University of Wichita, 1945; Elmo Roper, "Popularity of Types of Radio Programs," *New York Herald Tribune*, October 25, 1945.
6. Appendix D, Tables 8 to 15.
7. Appendix B, Questions 4B and 4C.

It is an interesting phenomenon that news media supplement rather than displace one another. This is not only true for radio and newspapers but also for other kinds of sources of information on current affairs. Take, for instance, the news weeklies such as *Time* and *Newsweek, Look* and *Life*. A variety of surveys have shown that the people who read these magazines are also the people who are more likely to listen to news commenators and to read more than one newspaper. By and large, the consumption of news from different sources is cumulative.[8]

It is worthwhile to speculate on two factors which may explain this rather general "law of news consumption." On the one hand, it is probably related to the specific nature of technological developments. The same trends which make for an ever larger variety of news sources make also for an ever larger amount of leisure time. The people, therefore, who are already interested in news, can satisfy their curiosity in a larger number of ways.

But the same social trends also make for greater literacy and greater interest in current affairs. Large sectors of the less educated population and hitherto uninterested women have newly entered the news market. They provide listeners to radio news without lessening the number of newspaper readers.

There is some evidence on this point in the present survey. The question was asked:

"From which one source do you get most of your daily news about what is going on—the newspapers or the radio?"

Table 12A gives the proportion of people who say radio rather than newspaper is their main source of news.

Radio is the favorite source for those groups in the population who presumably are the ones whose interest in news has been more recently developed. It is certainly fair to say that

---

8. For more details see Paul F. Lazarsfeld, "The Daily Newspaper and Its Competitors," *The Annals of the American Academy of Political and Social Science,* January, 1942, Vol. 219, pp. 32-43; and *Radio and the Printed Page,* New York: Duell, Sloan and Pearce, 1940, Chapter 5.

radio has contributed greatly to developing this new interest among women and less educated people and thus has done a great service to democracy's need for an informed population.

Table 12A

PROPORTION GETTING MOST DAILY NEWS FROM RADIO ACCORDING TO SEX AND EDUCATION[a]

	Men	Women
College	39%	56%
High school	55	64
Grammar school	62	72

[a] Appendix D, Table 16.

Few criticisms are volunteered against news programs.[9] To the specific question, "In what ways do you think radio news could be improved?", 40 per cent of the respondents volunteered suggestions. The chief complaint on the content of the newscasts themselves was against the brevity and lack of details of radio news.[10]

It is in the nature of broadcasting that any subject matter can only be given a limited amount of time. The only thing which can be done is to change the relative amount of time allocated to different topics. The survey, therefore, added another specific question:

"As far as your own listening is concerned, is the radio giving too much time, about the right amount, or not enough time to—news about other countries,—news about this country,—news about things around here?"

9. Appendix B, Question 17.
10. Appendix B, Question 5.

Table 13

SATISFACTION WITH FOREIGN, NATIONAL AND LOCAL NEWS

	Other countries	NEWS OF This country	Things around here
Not enough	17%	27%	33%
About right	64	66	57
Too much	10	2	2
No opinion	9	5	8
Total	100%	100%	100%

It is characteristic that the people who are likely to complain about too little foreign news are also the same ones who want more national and local news items on the air.[11] The complaints about the scarcity of local news are the most frequent. There seems to be an indicated need for more expansion of such local service. But the collection of local news items presents a serious problem to the local stations. While they get foreign news delivered by wire services, they would have to set up special machinery to track down happenings in the immediate area in which they are situated. Nonetheless, the finding that local news programs are a desired feature suggests that perhaps appropriate sponsorship might be attracted to defray costs of such an expanded service.[12]

Only 12 per cent of the respondents complain of inaccuracy or bias in the news. This is interesting because the question of balanced news treatment over the air is frequently raised among students of communications problems. Most of these

11. Appendix D, Table 17.
12. C. H. Sandage, *Radio Advertising for Retailers*, Cambridge, Mass.: Harvard University Press, 1945.

discussions are handicapped by a complete lack of statistical evidence as to the content of news programs and the opinions which commentators and news analysts express. While at the moment, the matter does not seem to present a real problem to the listeners themselves, there might very well develop critical situations in which the question of unbiased news would loom very high in the listeners' minds.[13] Actually it would be possible and perhaps desirable for the industry to provide some kind of periodic report on a sample of news bulletins and commentator programs which go out over the air. By providing such a service, the industry could anticipate and meet any such criticism if and when it arose. Such evidence could also be used to evaluate the balance obtained among different types of news.

Comedy and Variety Shows

Another type of program which appeals to all population groups for evening listening is comedy. It is usually taken as a matter of course that everyone likes a good laugh, and therefore, this category of program has rarely, if ever, been made an object of specific study.

Still there are a number of points about comedy programs which deserve further attention. Simply because the appeal seems so obvious, it would be interesting to find out why there is still a considerable minority of people who don't enjoy listening to them. (They seem to have a slightly lower appeal to farmers and residents of small towns; this might, however, be due to the many references to Hollywood and other "cosmopolitan" subject matters which are such handy topics for jokes, but which might be alien to some sectors of the country).[14]

Also, there is the interesting fact that so many of these programs show one characteristic pattern. The comedian, the hero of the program, is the butt of the jokes either by self-derision

13. See next chapter, page 88.
14. Appendix D, Tables 8 to 15.

or through his stooges. Is this a general function of humor or is it especially characteristic of the contemporaneous American scene?

There is very little satire on American programs. A few comedians use their programs to show up prejudices, or move more or less timidly in the direction of social criticism. But the great educational power which satire could have and has had at certain turns of literary history is certainly not fully utilized by present programs. It is perhaps no coincidence that the most plain-spoken, facetious character in American broadcasting is a dummy. While these topics go beyond the scope of the present report, they are certainly worth more attention than they get now by social psychologists and students of the arts.

Music

There is one kind of program which has an audience about as large as news, and that is music. This is not surprising if one knows that about half of all radio programs are of a musical nature. But here is a first concrete example of what has been referred to in the foregoing as "The Broadcasters' Dilemma."

Table 14

PROPORTION LIKING TO LISTEN TO POPULAR MUSIC IN DIFFERENT AGE GROUPS[a]

Age	Per cent
Under 30	72%
30 to 39	50
40 to 49	41
50 and over	22

[a] Appendix D, Table 10.

The list of programs submitted to the respondents included three types of musical programs; popular music, classical music and what was termed "old familiar music." Seventy-six per cent like some kind of music on the radio, but tastes in different types of music differ widely.[15] Popular music is liked overwhelmingly by young people. As a matter of fact, there are few program preferences which reveal such sharp variations as the age differences shown in Table 14.

Seventy-two per cent of the people below 30 years of age like to listen to popular music, but only 22 per cent of those over 50 years of age exhibit the same preference. No other factor plays nearly as large a role as age. There is a slight tendency for rural people to like popular music less, but education seems to make little difference.[16]

The taste for classical music, on the other hand, is mainly a function of environmental factors—education, and (to a lesser extent) whether people live in a metropolitan or rural environ-

Table 15

PROPORTION LIKING TO LISTEN TO CLASSICAL MUSIC IN THE EVENING BY SIZE OF TOWN AND EDUCATION[a]

	College	High school	Grammar school
Cities 100,000 and over	62%	35%	29%
Towns 2,500 to 100,000	50	35	22
Under 2,500 and farms	49	24	12

[a] For details see Appendix D, Table 14.

15. Appendix D, Table 18.
16. Appendix D, Tables 8 to 15.

ment. Table 15 shows that about two-thirds of the respondents who live in a big city and have gone to college like to listen to classical music; but only about a tenth of the people who have only had grammar school education and live in places with less than 2,500 population express this preference. (Age and sex play only a minor role.) [16a]

The last two tables contain information which goes beyond the immediate purpose of this discussion. They constitute good examples of the kind of contribution which radio research can make to a general knowledge of human affairs. There seem to be program tastes which vary strongly with age but are fairly independent of the environment in which people live. Other preferences are mainly determined by social factors and not by what one might call more biological contexts. The sharp rhythms and probably also the lyrics of the typical song hit may lose their meaning for people as they grow older and presumably become less concerned with the romantic aspects of life. The taste for classical music, on the other hand, is developed largely through external stimulation. If a person has gone to a school where he was exposed to the fine arts, or if he lives in an environment providing an opportunity to listen to good music, where people are likely to talk about it, or where there are other social rewards attached to music appreciation, then classical music on the radio finds in him a grateful listener.

Here are two examples of two rather different functions which radio must perform in the same general area. If so many young people want to hear popular music, they should be entitled to it. The broadcasters cannot be expected to deny the needs which nature and society develop in young people. But at the same time, radio has another function. It can help to reenforce and to develop elements of taste which are instilled in people by the more sophisticated environment which the schools and the artistic facilities of the big city develop. Here radio not only fulfills a need of certain individuals, but it also

---

16a. Appendix D, Tables 8, 10, 12, 15.

facilitates cultural efforts made by advanced groups in the community.[17]

For later reference, one further finding is recorded here. When people were asked what programs they would like to hear more on the radio, requests for music went far above all others. True, 59 per cent had no specific requests. But 16 per cent—over a quarter of those who did feel the need for more of any kind of programs—asked for more music. And one-half of these specifically stated they would like more serious music on the air. On the other hand, when asked what kinds of programs they would like to hear fewer of, 10 per cent mentioned music, most of whom were opposed to jazz.[18]

One word might be added about the role of "old familiar music." Forty-seven per cent of all respondents like to listen to this program type in the evening. This is probably a term which means a great variety of different things depending on the listener's interpretation. To an immigrant, it may mean Strauss waltzes; to a western farmer, cowboy songs; to others it may include hymns. Thus, it is understandable that no clear-cut audience listener differences can be found in such a heterogeneous category. It is somewhat more popular among older people.[19] Regional differences did not appear, but concealed within this catch-all category may be wide regional differences in the kinds of "familiar music" that are most popular in each area. Thus this kind of radio fare is eminently suited for local and regional programming.

Daytime Serials

The popularity of news programs, comedians and music has already been discussed. There is a fourth type of program

17. This mutual interaction between program supply and educational efforts in the field of good music has been studied and demonstrated in a detailed study by Edward Suchman, "Invitation to Music," *Radio Research, 1941*, by Paul F. Lazarsfeld and Frank N. Stanton, New York: Duell, Sloan and Pearce, 1941, pp. 140-188.
18. Appendix B, Questions 13 and 14.
19. Appendix D, Tables 8 to 15.

which is also among the most popular on the air—dramatic programs. And here radio has developed a form of its own: the serial dramatization. An intensive discussion of these daytime serials as over the last few years yielded a considerable amount of literature, the conclusions of which are too well known to require repetition here.[20] In the present context attention is focused chiefly on the character of the audience to this type of program.

The available feminine daytime audience is fairly evenly divided into those who do and those who do not listen to serial stories. If they do, they are likely to be fans and to listen to an average of about four a day; if they don't they are frequently violent opponents.

Listeners to daytime serials are the most thoroughly studied and best known sector of the radio audience.

Thorough efforts have been made to find out what differences exist between women who do and do not listen to serials.[21] The strange thing is that very few variables could be found among two groups of women who have such opposite listening tastes. In practically all the psychological and social characteristics which have been investigated, the two groups are virtually alike.

Only two major differences have been discovered. One is educational. Table 16 shows that the lower in the educational scale a woman is, the more is she inclined to say she likes to listen to daytime serials.

---

20. For a summary and general discussion of daytime serials see *Education on the Air, Fourteenth Yearbook of the Institute for Education by Radio*, Columbus, Ohio: Ohio State University, 1943, pp. 343-355.
21. *Radio's Daytime Serial*, New York: Columbia Broadcasting System, Inc., September, 1945; and Paul F. Lazarsfeld and Frank N. Stanton, *Radio Research 1942-1943*, New York: Duell, Sloan and Pearce, 1944, pp. 3-33. Other studies made by the Blue Network and the National Broadcasting Company have corroborated these results. The agreement between a variety of studies is one of the most encouraging episodes in the field of communication research. See Appendix D, Tables 12 and 13.

Table 16

PROPORTION OF WOMEN
ON DIFFERENT EDUCATIONAL LEVELS
LIKING TO LISTEN TO SERIAL STORIES[a]

	Per cent
College	26%
High school	38
Grammar school	41

[a] Appendix D, Table 12.

This result has led to many conclusions that serial listeners differ markedly in other respects from non-serial listeners. The fact of the matter is that if serial listeners are compared with other women on the same general cultural level, it is virtually impossible to find significant differences between them.

But even the fact that there are educational differences requires a qualification. People's attitudes toward daytime serials can be measured by three indices: their listening habits, their expressed preferences, and by their criticisms. All studies have shown that the educational differences in listening are small. Women with a grade school education and those with high school, listen to serials in about the same amounts; only on the college level is there somewhat less listening to serials. Preference data of the kind reported in Table 16 show only a modicum of relationship to education. Criticism, on the other hand, is most susceptible to educational differences. Each successive grade of education achieved makes for more critics.

This would suggest an interesting generalization on the role which sophistication plays in people's attitudes toward radio. Its influence is greatest when they are explicitly called upon to express criticism. Educational groups differ in their general preferences, but not as much as when a critical frame of reference is invoked. Differences in actual listening are small probably because the existing supply of programs is at least as important a factor as the attitudes of the listeners.

Table 17

DIFFERENCES BETWEEN SERIAL AND NON-SERIAL LISTENERS IN RADIO-MINDEDNESS

		Serial listeners	Non-serial listeners
Usual amount of evening radio listening:			
Less than 2 hours		34%	47%
2 or 3 hours		49	42
4 or more hours		17	11
	Total women	100%	100%
From which source do you get most of your daily news:			
Newspapers		21%	35%
Radio		74	60
No preference		5	5
	Total women	100%	100%

The other difference between listeners and opponents to daytime serials is what might be called their radio-mindedness. In many respects the serial listeners are more interested in radio and consider it their favorite medium of mass communication.

The present survey furnished two characteristic examples. The woman who usually listens to several serials during the day is still more inclined to listen to the radio in the evening than other women. And when it comes to the question of whether they get most of their news from newspapers or radio, the choice of the serial fans is clearly on radio's side. The differences shown in Table 17 hold true irrespective of the respondent's educational level.[22]

All these differences are quite small. The basic fact remains that women are divided evenly for and against one of the most characteristic creations of American radio—the daytime serial. Here, is the broadcasters' dilemma in its full force.

Learning from the Radio

The discussion of the daytime serial highlights the problems which radio meets in the field of mass culture. Similar dilemmas arose in other mass media as they expanded in the course of recent technological and commercial developments. The comics, Hollywood, the book clubs have all been the objects of the same sort of attacks that plague daytime radio. But the airways face an additional controversy which has been raging since its early days. What is radio's educational function?

All parties concerned seem to agree on the basic issue that radio has an educational responsibility. Programs such as the Chicago Round Table, the American School of the Air, the Cavalcade of America, the Philharmonic broadcasts and many others have become classics among American programs.[23]

But how far this educational function should go is by no means settled. On the one hand, a variety of civic groups interested in education and other cultural activities have steadily pressed for more and better educational programs. On the

---

22. Appendix D, Table 19. Also *Attitudes of Rural People toward Radio Service*, U. S. Dept. of Agriculture, BAE, Nov., 1945, pp. 28-32.
23. For summary of educational broadcasting, see: Carroll Atkinson, *Radio Network Contributions to Education*, Boston: Meador Pub. Co., 1942.

other hand, in the past Congress and the Federal Communications Commission have, after considerable debate, declined to rule on any fixed amount of time that stations are required to give to educational programs. A portent for the future, however, perhaps lies in the fact that a fifth of the FM channels have recently been reserved for educational broadcasting.

It would certainly facilitate the whole problem if there were more information available on the uses to which radio is put by its audience. More should be known about those who definitely want to use radio for their self-improvement. It is difficult to say how many would listen more to serious programs in addition to news, if they were provided in larger numbers and with greater regularity. In a supplementary inquiry,[24] a sample of 498 respondents was asked two pertinent questions. One read as follows:

> "Besides news, do you think it is important for a radio station to have at least one serious or educational program every evening, or doesn't it matter?"

Seventy-four per cent of the respondents answered in the affirmative. This result is obviously open to one major objection. People can easily approve of educational programs without being prospective listeners themselves.

In order to see beyond such perfunctory approval of an educational stereotype, a "tighter" question was asked. The wording of the question and the distribution of answers are shown in Table 18.

Only six per cent answered the third alternative. With judgment sharpened by this result, it would appear now that the wording of the third alternative was too strict. It would probably have been more realistic to phrase it thus: "I am very much interested in serious or educational programs and wish there were more of them."

It is fairly safe to say that about half of the population, as

24. See Appendix C.

things stand now, do not use radio as an educational device; but for how many people radio has a serious educational function, and how many are at least potential listeners of this kind is difficult to say.[25]

Table 18

PURPOSES TO WHICH PEOPLE PUT RADIO

"Which of the following best describes the way you yourself use the radio?"	Per cent
"I may get the news from the radio, but otherwise I use it only for entertainment"	46%
"Besides the news and entertainment, I like to listen to some serious or educational programs once in awhile"	46
"I listen mostly to serious programs or educational programs and wish there were more of them"	6
No opinion	2
Total	100%

The whole discussion of radio's educational function meets with still another difficulty. What is an educational program? Even educators do not limit their definitions to the broadcasting of classroom lectures. Much fruitful experimentation made during the last fifteen years has broadened the concept considerably.[26] The question can even be raised as to whether

25. Research in this direction would be very desirable but not easy. The right approach would be to ask half a dozen pertinent questions in a variety of wordings and then draw reasoned inferences from the results and their interrelationships. A similar problem came up and was well solved by the Army when, during the war, it was important to find out how many returning veterans would want to go to school. See Louis Guttman, "A Basis for Scaling Qualitative Data," *American Sociological Review*, Vol. 9, 1944, pp. 139-150. See this text, pp. 15-20, for similar approach.

26. The reader will find much valuable information in the yearly reports on the meetings of the Institute for Education by Radio in Columbus, Ohio, *Education Over the Air*.

the efforts to make education palatable have gone too far. Historical dramatizations which spend a large proportion of their time on sound effects and trivial personal angles might be fine in their intentions but poor in their results.

The present survey was not designed primarily to determine how radio can raise the level of public information and interest, but it does give some idea of what the people themselves think they do learn from the radio. The question was asked:

"Aside from news, in what other fields does the radio add to your information or knowledge?"

Only 25 per cent say they have never learned anything from the radio. The type of information people claim to have acquired is shown in Table 19.

There are a number of interesting leads visible in this table. Almost a third of the respondents refer to information which is of practical use in their daily work. They are largely housewives or farmers.

It is not surprising that women homemakers are the ones who now profit most from radio. As an audience, they can be reached during the day at a time when the men cannot listen. To a certain degree, a similar situation prevails with farmers. They can be reached at noon and early in the morning when most of the urban population is still asleep.

This result implies another serious difficulty confronting the broadcaster. There can be little doubt that radio can bring useful knowledge to many special interest groups. It is easy to visualize stamp collectors and dog lovers listening avidly to program after program on their chosen avocations. The difficulty is that there are so many of these relatively small groups that a mass medium can give each only a very little time. Perhaps in the future when there are many more stations in existence as a result of the expansion of frequency modulation

(FM) broadcasting, more of the program content may be devoted to special interest groups in a manner similar to specialized magazines today.

Table 19

FIELDS IN WHICH RADIO HAS ADDED TO LISTENERS' INFORMATION OR KNOWLEDGE

		Per cent[a]
General Knowledge		67%
Politics, current events or history	22%	
Quiz programs	15	
Religion	5	
Science and medicine	4	
Geography	2	
Art or literature	2	
Vocabulary or speech	2	
Miscellaneous or general	15	
Practical Information		31%
Homemaking, cooking or shopping information	22%	
Agricultural information	9	
Enjoyment or Cultural Information		25%
Music	16%	
Drama	5	
Sports	4	
Don't Learn or Listen Only for Entertainment		25%

[a] Percentages add to more than 100% because more than one answer per person was possible.

Two-thirds of the people say radio has added to their general knowledge, which to many an educator might be an unexpected finding. The traditional topics of our educational system, geography, science, etc., are mentioned by relatively few respondents. There are three program types from which people seem to learn most frequently: discussion of public affairs, quiz programs, and religious programs. It seems as if radio listeners have developed their own educational world, different from the world of formal education but appropriate to the nature of this medium.

Interestingly enough, these three types of programs are in the forefront in still another context. In the supplementary inquiry mentioned above (page 54) the following question was asked:

"Can you give me an example of a program now on the air which you think of as a serious or an educational program?"

The three program types listed most frequently are forums, mentioned by 21 per cent; quiz programs, by 16 per cent; and religious programs, by 8 per cent.[27] On each of these three, some additional observations are worth mentioning.

Forums. There is general agreement that the discussion of public affairs is one of the most distinctive and impressive features of the American system of broadcasting. If the advantages and disadvantages of the European system of governmental control are considered without prejudice, the differences on this score are striking. Nowhere in Europe is there any approach to the amount of public discussion which exists on the radio in this country. Apparently no government controlled radio has been able to tolerate such open discussions to the same extent. While steady vigilance is needed to keep these American programs free from direct or indirect restrictions imposed by commercial considerations or influences, the very fact that they exist and play such a large role is probably

27. For the full list, see Appendix D, Table 20.

the best argument that can be advanced for the American system.

Inversely, listening to this kind of program can be used as a gauge of the depths of penetration of concern for public affairs which is so important for the working of a democracy. Tables 20 and 21 have been devised to yield some evidence on this point. Men and women have been divided into those above and below 40 years of age, and according to whether they have completed high school or not. Table 20 shows the proportion of respondents who like to listen to talks and discussions of public issues.

Table 20

PROPORTION LIKING TO LISTEN TO TALKS AND DISCUSSIONS ON PUBLIC ISSUES ACCORDING TO AGE, SEX AND EDUCATION [a]

	HIGH SCHOOL GRADUATION OR MORE		LESS THAN HIGH SCHOOL GRADUATION	
	Under 40	40 and over	Under 40	40 and over
Men	48%	59%	31%	46%
Women	38%	48%	20%	34%

[a] For details see Appendix D, Table 21.

Table 21 gives the proportion in each group that reports that they have learned something from such programs.

The two tables show that much is still to be done to instill a widespread interest in public affairs. It is not surprising that people with the least education are least interested. But for many a reader the marked differences between men and women will be a painful finding. Especial attention should be given to the age differences. The younger people in this country are less concerned with public affairs than the older.[28]

Table 21

PROPORTION SAYING THEY
HAVE LEARNED POLITICS OR CURRENT
EVENTS FROM THE RADIO
ACCORDING TO AGE, SEX AND EDUCATION[a]

	HIGH SCHOOL GRADUATION OR MORE		LESS THAN HIGH SCHOOL GRADUATION	
	Under 40	40 and over	Under 40	40 and over
Men	30%	40%	20%	21%
Women	22%	30%	8%	15%

[a] For details see Appendix D, Table 21.

Quiz Programs. These are among the most popular entertainment in the evening radio schedule. People say they like to listen to quizzes about as frequently as they mention liking radio drama or comedy programs. Fifty-three per cent of all radio listeners in the present survey list quiz programs among their favorite types of radio programs.

But many listeners feel that they are also a source of knowledge. An early qualitative study found that listeners get a variety of competitive, self-rating and sporting gratifications out of quiz programs.[29] But the educational appeal was the one

[28] For a similar result and a discussion of its implications, see Paul F. Lazarsfeld, Bernard Berelson and Hazel Gaudet, *The People's Choice*, New York: Duell, Sloan and Pearce, 1944, p. 45.
[29] Herta Herzog, "Professor Quiz—A Gratification Study," in *Radio and the Printed Page* by Paul F. Lazarsfeld, New York: Duell, Sloan and Pearce, 1940, pp. 64-93.

most universally stressed by all listeners. While admitting quizzes were enjoyable and entertaining, they nonetheless considered them educational. Most respondents said they got diversified knowledge from quiz programs. They were learning bits of information which some day might increase their social status if brought up in a conversation. Although some admitted that the information thus gained was scattered and unorganized, they seemed to feel that if the subject ever did come up, they would remember what they had learned and be able to apply it.

Would it be possible to turn this effective technique to good account for more educational purposes? Quizzes were developed by entertainers and largely ignored by educators. Only occasionally does one hear a quiz on books or on history. But their popularity among all groups in the population attests to the fact that it is a program type which could more often be employed by the educational experts. It is accepted modern educational practice to pay attention to the motivation of the learner. Now the challenge of the question-and-answer program offers a decided spur to listeners. There is then no reason why some of the heterogeneity of the usual quiz could not be supplanted by an integrated content. Educators and radio producers should work together to develop this technique.

Somewhat related to quiz programs are the audience participation shows which have recently gained considerable listener acceptance. They are similar to quizzes in that a master of ceremonies talks to people in the studio audience, although the content does not deal with knowledge questions but with facts about the interviewed persons themselves. It happens that few data on audience participation programs are available from this study.[30] There are other unpublished studies, however, which throw some light on the appeals such programs have for listeners. Like the daytime serials they focus on ordinary people

[30] See Appendix D, Table 9 for some information on the general popularity of audience participation shows.

in circumstances similar to the listeners, but they do it in a less dramatic and less emotional way. There is a considerable group of women who avoid listening to daytime serials because of their "upsetting" qualities, who want programs from which they can remain more psychologically aloof than they can from serials. It is quite likely that those women who enjoy hearing about people like themselves but do not want to get too involved are the ones who like to listen to audience participation programs. There is also another factor which may in part account for the popularity of audience participation shows. They have no day-to-day continuity and hence are not as demanding of regular listening as are continued serial stories. This seems to be an advantage for a number of listeners.

Religious Programs. Thirty-five per cent of the women

Table 22

PROPORTION LIKING TO LISTEN
TO RELIGIOUS PROGRAMS IN THE EVENING
ACCORDING TO AGE AND EDUCATION[a]

	College	High school	Grammar school
Under 30	8%	11%	13%
30 to 39	12	15	19
40 to 49	9	16	22
50 and over	16	28	33

[a] For details see Appendix D, Table 15.

interviewed say they like to listen to some form of devotional program in the daytime. Twenty per cent of both men and women listeners enjoy religious broadcasts in the evening. The audience pattern of devotional programs is quite different from anything else in the radio scene. Table 22 makes it clear that the older and the less educated a population group is, the more will they be likely to listen to religious programs. Religious broadcasts are also more popular in smaller towns and farm areas.[31]

It is interesting that so many listeners consider religious programs as a source of learning. Obviously, for people who read little, a sermon is a useful way to get guidance in some of their problems. As a matter of fact, for the less educated groups, religious programs seem to be so important that they feel they don't get enough of them on the radio. The following question was asked:

"Are there any kinds of programs you'd like to hear more of?"

A detailed listing of the responses is given in the Appendix.[32] For the present purpose only a few programs pertinent to the present discussion were singled out for presentation:

Table 23

A FEW DIFFERENCES BETWEEN EDUCATIONAL LEVELS IN WHAT PEOPLE WANT TO HEAR MORE OF ON RADIO

	College	High school	Grammar school
Classical music	16%	8%	4%
Information programs	8	4	2
Religious programs	3	2	8

31. Appendix D, Table 22.
32. Appendix D, Table 23.

In this context religious programs lead all others for the less educated people. As a matter of fact, the proportion of those on the college level who want more informational programs is exactly the same as the proportion of those on the grammar school level who want more religious programs. Perhaps no other table would be more suited to end a chapter which was devoted to showing what diversified gratifications people get from radio and how difficult it is, therefore, to satisfy them all. The discussion will now turn to some concrete consequences attendant upon this state of affairs.

Chapter IV. THE CRITIC, THE PEOPLE
AND THE INDUSTRY

STUDYING RADIO IS LIKE HIKING IN MOUN-
tainous country. The climber thinks that once he
reaches the top the landscape will lie revealed before him. But
when he achieves his objective he finds another peak ahead
spurring him to further effort. Mountain climbing presents
a never ending challenge.

This report now finds itself in a similar situation. Three
major findings have thus far emerged: the American audience
presents a complex variety of listener interests; advertising is
a necessary but nonetheless troublesome economic foundation
of broadcasting; the industry has coped with this vexing net of
problems with some success. From any viewpoint the critics
and dissatisfied listeners seem definitely in the minority.

But the time for relaxation and enjoyment of the view must
be postponed for one more question: Who are the critics?
While this constitutes a somewhat complicated subject for
analysis, the answer can be stated quite simply: the critical
voices come chiefly from the articulate strata of the community. They come from the people who are likely to be heard
and to attract attention beyond the size of the group they
represent. To demonstrate this fact, a short discussion is inserted on the stratification of the American community.

Social Stratification and Criticism

Everyone knows that some people have more power, more
prestige, and more money than others. The difference between
the underdog and the man in the social register is a well-known
feature of daily life. There is disagreement on the extent to
which these social strata are fixed in the American community.

Some consider the classes of society are now fairly well established and rigid, while others think that many of the "little men" still have a chance to become big shots. The corner grocer in a small community sometimes has more prestige with his fellow men than the rich manufacturer. But by and large, it is widely recognized that society looks like a seven layer cake, and there is not much doubt, at least, as to who is on the top and who is at the bottom.

The research student is also aware of social stratification. He expects to find more magazines, more refrigerators and more Republicans in the upper strata; more children, more unemployment and more Democrats in the lower strata.

It does not make much difference which particular index is used to classify people into social layers. Any one of the four or five reasonably good measures shows about the same results in a survey such as the present one. For a number of reasons, education is used as an index of stratification in the following discussion. The people interviewed are divided into those who have not gone beyond grade school; those who have attended high school; and the third and top layer consists of people who have had at least some college. For the country as a whole, about 55 per cent belong in the lowest level and about 12 per cent belong in the highest.[1]

Now who are the critics? The survey shows that less educated people are the least critical of radio in all of its aspects. Take, for example, this question: "Do you ever feel like criticizing when you listen to the radio?" Twenty-three per cent of the college people, 31 per cent of the high school people, but 49 per cent of the grade school people have no criticisms. And so it goes all through the survey: the lower a person stands

1. For the more statistically minded readers see Appendix D, Table 24. It shows, for example, that among the less educated people, 50 per cent belong to the "D" type, as ascertained by the interviewers' ratings. But among the highly educated people, only 7 per cent are "D" people. So an educational classification and a classification by interviewers' ratings are really quite interchangeable. And the Appendix also proves that all our subsequent findings would have been statistically similar whether we used the one or the other to classify people into social strata.

THE CRITIC, THE PEOPLE AND THE INDUSTRY 67

in the social pyramid, the less likely he is to express criticism and the more inclined he is to approve of radio as it is now.[1a] The evidence on this point is combined in one table. In Table 24 six questions are listed on which a respondent could give critical comment. The figures indicate for each of the three strata, the proportion of respondents who say they have no criticism to make. It is quite startling to see how consistently dissatisfaction becomes higher as education increases.

Table 24

PROPORTION WHO ARE UNCRITICAL OF RADIO ON DIFFERENT EDUCATIONAL LEVELS

	College	High school	Grammar school
Proportion who like or "don't mind" advertising on the radio	57%	65%	72%
Proportion who prefer radio produced with advertising	54	62	71
Proportion who make no suggestions for the improvement of radio news	41	59	70
Proportion who know of no kinds of programs they'd like fewer of on the air	37	52	67
Proportion who say they do not ever feel like criticizing the radio	23	31	49
Proportion who do not feel strongly about any of the listed criticisms of radio commercials	13	21	40

1a. A similar relation between education and the critical faculty probably exists in most areas—not in the field of radio alone.

This finding is probably the result of a variety of factors. For one thing, the person in the lowest group is most likely to accept things as they are. Because he never had much formal education, he has not acquired the training which enables him to look critically at his environment.

There is also the special situation arising out of the survey itself. The poor fellow has less facility as a reader and talker, and therefore, on a check list or in a free answer question he produces fewer replies. His lack of criticism might well be exaggerated by the survey situation.[2]

While the weight of poverty makes some people meek and lack of education keeps their critical faculties from developing, there is still another factor which is most important in explaining why the lower strata voice so much less objection to radio. After all, radio is a mass medium. The greatest part of the population belongs to the group which has been classified here as less educated. Through program ratings and through common sense the broadcaster knows what the large majority of people like and, as a result, this majority is actually more suited by the radio offerings than the more highly educated minority. The latter, through formal education and a more fortunate course of life, have acquired a greater sophistication of taste, a greater range of experience, and more initiative in choosing what is to their liking. It is the more articulate and the intellectually more mobile person who is more likely to be critical of radio.

2. There is some evidence on this point in Table 24. In one question it will be seen that less educated people are more likely to say that they would not prefer radio without advertising. The difference between college and grade school people is 17%. But in another question people are asked to check some of the ten criticisms of radio presented to them on the list. Again many more grade school people than college people check none: here the difference is 27%. Probably, in addition to being more satisfied, some of the lower educated people also try to avoid reading the list. A similar piece of evidence is given in Appendix D, Table 25. The less educated people, although they listen to the radio more, mention fewer programs as their favorites.

The Role of the Broadcaster

Whatever the reasons are, the fact remains that the more articulate strata of the population, the people who can take the individual broadcaster to task because they have influence and prestige in the circles in which he moves, are most likely to be critical of his work. This puts the broadcaster in a difficult position because he knows from his daily experience that the bulk of his listeners are quite satisfied with what he is offering them. How can the requirements of the intellectual *avant garde* be reconciled with those of the large majority of the less demanding members of the community?

To raise the question at all might at first glance appear to be questioning the basic tenet of democracy. Shouldn't the majority always rule? But in matters of taste and culture such a simplified application of the democratic principle has never been considered seriously. The men who enforced compulsory schooling on reluctant communities are today heroic figures.

For a moment it might look as if we are here facing the conflict of two basic principles both of which are dear to the American tradition: the belief in the common man; and the conviction that in cultural matters the experts who see a problem in its broader context, should get a preferential hearing. But actually, the conflict is neither new nor unexpected nor tragic, for a third facet of the American tradition resolves it. As a matter of fact, this third idea—that of checks and balances —was developed precisely to meet such conflicts. In this country institutions have been allowed to change, improve and progress but under the guarantee that all parties concerned would have an ample opportunity to be heard and to have their interests defended. In the American radio scene the conciliation of opposing forces presents itself as follows: on the one side stands the advertiser whose main interest is to reach as large a number of people as possible. The educational structure of the country being what it is, most advertisers will inevitably want to promote programs which conform to the understanding and taste of the larger and less educated sectors of the population. On the other side stands the critic. He wants a more sophisticated radio for a variety of reasons. It might be that in his profession he has developed certain standards of taste which he is eager to see disseminated. Or he may be guided by a social philosophy: he may think radio makes too much profit, or he may feel that commercialized radio is "opium for the masses." To such people may be added those in the upper strata who merely want to have radio more to their own listening taste.

The advertiser has on his side his economic power and, to say the least, the acquiescence of the majority of the people. The critic has on his side the ability to talk and to write, and the moral approval which goes with any intensive expression of an idea. The broadcaster is called upon to compromise between these forces and to find ever new solutions in his daily work.

The Communications Act places the final responsibility for conduct of the station upon the broadcaster and with it the obligation for the development of radio as a whole. One of the responsibilities of the licensee is undoubtedly to be alert to the voice of the critic, to balance his suggestions against other available information, and to translate into action the resulting conclusion. The present survey is an example of this process. Here is a trade association of the industry going out to the listener to invite his criticism of radio on a number of vital issues. Other sources of guidance are the daily observations of the broadcaster and his staff and the scrutiny of current literature. Conferences of educators and other groups are also useful sources of suggestions.

Because one survey cannot possibly cover all aspects of radio, it might be useful at this point to give a brief summary of what the main topics of discussion are in the radio field at the moment. At some points the present survey makes some contribution. At other points, future surveys are indicated, and at still others a totally different approach than that offered by a public opinion poll would be needed to provide pertinent information.

The Five Pillars of Radio Criticism

The problems of radio as an institution have varied with its development. Twenty years ago listeners were absorbed in tuning to as many distant stations as possible. Today this is no longer of vital interest to most of the radio audiences. In fifty years perhaps, the intrusion upon privacy by an electronic eye which reaches into every corner may become the outstanding problem of radio. At this moment, the main topics of discussion seem to be centered around five points.

(a) *Advertising.* The attitudes of a cross-section of the population to radio commercials were discussed in Chapter II. There is much controversial literature available on the general role which advertising plays in modern society. It would transcend the scope of this report to extend the discussion of this vast subject.

(b) *Radio as an Educational Device.* In Chapter III (page 53) some data on the problem of learning over the radio has been discussed. It was pointed out that there is not yet conclusive evidence as to the number of people who are ready to use radio for the purpose of self-education. But there is one aspect in the results of this survey (and previous findings of this kind) which deserves special attention. The people who are more susceptible to radio education are those who need it less. It is also probably true that the range of their interests and the demands upon their time afford them less opportunity to listen to the radio. It will be remembered that the respondents were asked whether they had learned anything in the course of their listening. Their replies reported in Table 25 could be classified in three major groups: general knowledge, practical information and enjoyment or cultural values. If these answers are tabulated separately for people on different educational levels, it is found that with the exception of practical information people with only a grammar school education are much less likely than others to gain knowledge from the radio.

Table 25

INFORMATION OTHER THAN NEWS LEARNED FROM THE RADIO BY PEOPLE ON DIFFERENT EDUCATIONAL LEVELS[a]

Learn from radio:	College	High school	Grammar school
General knowledge	94%	68%	49%
Practical information	23	35	30
Enjoyment or cultural information	33	28	17
Don't learn or listen only for entertainment	14	20	36

[a] Percentages add to more than 100% because more than one answer per person was possible.

Table 25 seems to indicate that a certain amount of formal training is needed before a listener is likely to derive other than entertainment or news values from the radio.[3] A similar conclusion can be derived from the subsidiary inquiry made with 498 listeners mentioned before. When these respondents were asked whether they used radio at all for anything other than news listening and entertainment, the affirmative answers were: 63 per cent among college people, 56 per cent among listeners with at least some high school and 43 per cent among those who had not gone beyond grade school.[4] This seems to indicate

3. See also Appendix D, Table 26.
4. Appendix D, Table 27.

THE CRITIC, THE PEOPLE AND THE INDUSTRY 73

that the general stage of intellectual development in which a country finds itself sets definite limits which radio does not have the power to transcend.

There is still a considerable range within which the broadcaster can operate.[4a] And he will be expected to operate on the upper limits of this range. The situation can be summed up as follows: few people want to learn by way of the radio, but most critics agree that they should. Therefore, the best thing for the broadcaster to do is to keep the volume of educational broadcasts slightly above what the masses want. In this way, he may contribute to a systemantic rise in the general cultural level without defeating the educational goal by driving the audience away. This policy will disappoint some educators and drive some listeners away, but it is precisely the kind of compromise solution which must be found.

There is, however, a real need for more continuous and systematic evaluation of the position of educational broadcasting. There should be periodic program surveys so that the interested parties can really know how many and what kind of educational programs are being broadcast. Because progress in educational radio will only result from perpetual interchange between educators and broadcasters, systematic data about the current status are highly desirable—and they certainly are not now in existence.

(c) *Access to the Air.* The whole broad problem of freedom of speech has changed greatly during the last 170 years. When the First Amendment was enacted, its main purpose was to safeguard the individual citizen against government interference. In the early days newspapers were few in number and of small circulation. Since then new means of mass communication have been born and developed—newspapers and magazines with millions of readers and radio stations with millions of listeners. And what is equally important mass communication has become big business. A network or a corporation

4a. This formulation was originally put forward by Lyman Bryson.

which publishes magazines selling in the millions may have as little intention of influencing people's thinking as has the manufacturer of refrigerators. But whether by commission or omission, no medium of communication can avoid influencing the mind.

As a result, freedom of speech is now a three-cornered proposition between the government, the communications industry and the individual citizen. The private person who wishes to express an idea still demands to be free from government interference. But he is also confronted by the problem of how to get access to the media of communication. In other words, he has to cope with two kinds of freedom of speech, a negative and a positive one. This, in turn, complicates the relations between government and the communications industry. The broadcaster has to maintain vigilance to see that the government does not interfere with the freedom of radio as an institution. But as a business man, he may sometimes meet the government in a different role. The government may interfere with the communication business because it was called upon by groups of private citizens to safeguard their freedom of speech.

The resultant problems are complicated by the unanticipated consequences which each move of the three parties could have. Private citizens might set into motion government interference directed towards the industry, which later on might boomerang against themselves. The industry might defend its commercial interest under the formula of freedom of speech to a point where the ideals of the First Amendment become discredited in the minds of the citizens and a vital tenet of democracy would lose its popular support.

Obviously this type of question cannot be settled by a public opinion poll. As a matter of fact, the present survey contains some material which shows the extent to which the majority of the people are *not* aware of the problems involved.

The sale of radio time for the soliciting of membership in various kinds of organizations is generally frowned upon by the industry. This is done as part of a general policy to keep the air free for people irrespective of whether they have money or not. In the survey under review, NORC asked:

> "Do you think that radio stations should sell time for the following things or should it give the time free or shouldn't they be on the air at all?"

The list of items submitted and the distribution of answers obtained are given in Table 26.

Table 26

PEOPLE'S FEELINGS AS TO THE USE OF TIME FOR THE SOLICITING OF MEMBERSHIP IN ORGANIZATIONS

	Give	Sell	Not on air	No opinion	Total per cent
To solicit Red Cross memberships	82%	8%	4%	6%	100%
To solicit Community Chest donations	78	8	6	8	100
Political broadcasts	7%	76%	9%	8%	100%
To solicit correspondence school registrations	9	60	15	16	100
To solicit members for businessmen's organizations	6	57	21	16	100
To solicit labor union memberships	7	42	36	15	100
To solicit funds for churches	57%	13%	22%	8%	100%

Table 26 suggests strongly that in answering this question people do not pass on the general policy problems involved as much as they express their attitudes toward the different organizations mentioned. People are favorably inclined toward the Red Cross and the Community Chest and therefore want to give them free time. The next four items refer to more mundane pursuits and therefore few expect radio to give free time to them. The decision here is made in terms of whether time should be sold for such purposes or whether such people should be on the air at all. Most people are so used to political broadcasts, that everyone agrees they should be on the air. The labor unions meet most opposition. On the other hand, attitudes toward the soliciting of funds for churches are ambivalent. Only a few people feel that time should be sold to religious groups. Those who think that time should be given probably have a reverent attitude toward churches. A considerable number, however, who are opposed to church solicitations on the air at all are possibly influenced by a few bad examples of small religious sects which have used the radio for mercenary purposes. People, then, seem little aware of the complicated problems implied in such questions and their answers seem to be given in a different frame of reference than the questions intended.

Public opinion should be the final judge on matters of policy only when all the pertinent facts have been widely discussed, so that it can be reasonably certain that interrogator and respondent are talking about the same thing. The same is probably true for most of the intricate aspects of the problem of freedom of the air.[5] It is very unlikely, for instance, that an individual listener has the background to judge whether news broadcasts and commentators give a fair and balanced picture of current events. Again the answer could only be approached if continuous records of the actual performance of the average radio station were available. There is no reason why, for

5. Hadley Cantril has shown that people who approve of freedom of speech would sometimes in the same public opinion poll say that Communists and Fascists should not be permitted to talk publicly. See *Gauging Public Opinion*, Princeton, N. J.: Princeton University Press, 1944, pp. 183-184.

example, there could not be a periodic sampling of commentator scripts to study the expressed opinion on a variety of matters for the whole industry. The same could be done with round-table discussions and with news bulletins. In recent years, and especially during the war, the techniques of content analysis have been so far developed that it will not be difficult to establish criteria of fairness in news bulletins and news commentaries.[6] A further important set of data could be gained if stations kept records on all requests for time, whether granted or refused.

The objection might be raised that such records would be too expensive. It is a question of how important one considers the topics on which records are being kept.[7] If questions of social performance are taken seriously, the provision of funds for continuous statistical checks would undoubtedly be worthwhile. Who should sponsor such periodic checks? They could be done by the National Association of Broadcasters, but then an advisory board of experts in commercial research should be created which would vouch for the techniques and for the selection of material. Or regional boards who, at the same time, might perform some of the other research and advisory functions such as those mentioned in this present monograph might be considered. During the war, draft, ration and similar boards were quite successful. It is worth considering to what extent they might play a role in some of the problems which agitate the radio world.[8]

Even the results of a detailed program analysis, of course,

6. Harold D. Lasswell, "Describing the Contents of Communications," in *Propaganda, Communications, and Public Opinion*, Princeton, N. J.: Princeton University Press, 1946, pp. 74-94.
7. Broadcast Music, Inc. which handles the payment of music royalties for the majority of American radio stations, keeps a monthly detailed analysis of a sampling of station reports which accounts for every single piece of music which is played over the air. There the expenses are carried as a matter of course by all parties commercially concerned.
8. See Paul F. Lazarsfeld, "The Effect of Radio on Public Opinion," in *Print, Radio and Film in a Democracy*, edited by Douglas Waples, Chicago: University of Chicago, 1942, pp. 77-78.

would not wholly speak for themselves. They would still have to be interpreted in the light of the whole problem of access to the air. It is an old request that all sides of a controversial issue should be heard, but it is never easy to say how many sides an issue has. Neither is it always easy to judge whether the selection of topics is biased or the result of sound judgment. But availability of data, as suggested here, would certainly place the discussion of these problems on a sounder basis.

While the whole complex of freedom of the air cannot be decided by asking a simple public opinion poll question, it is still interesting to know what the general public thinks is the situation at the moment. The following question was asked in the present survey:

"I'd like to ask you how fair you think radio stations, newspapers and magazines generally are. For example, do you think radio stations are generally fair in giving both sides of an argument? How about newspapers in general? Magazines?"

The distribution of answers is given in Table 27.

Table 27

ATTITUDES TOWARD FAIRNESS OF RADIO STATIONS, NEWSPAPERS AND MAGAZINES

	Radio stations	Magazines	Newspapers
Fair	81%	45%	39%
Not fair	8	22	49
Don't know	11	33	12
Total	100%	100%	100%

Most listeners are of the opinion that radio is fair in handling controversial issues. As a matter of fact, if one realizes how many listeners would individually disagree with the opinions expressed by certain commentators, it is quite impressive. Viewing the radio scheme as a whole, 81 per cent feel that most radio stations make serious efforts to be fair to all sides.

The figures pertaining to the other two media should not be used for invidious comparisons. Newspapers, after all, in the American tradition, are entitled to editorial opinion and they do not claim to present both sides of every argument. In magazines, the straight editorial content is small and many people might not even be aware that magazines have editorial pages or editorial policies. Therefore, in regard to the other two media, additional questions might have to be asked to put the comparison on a sound footing. The present question just goes to show that barring more analytical evidence to the contrary, the public has an impression that both sides of an argument are usually presented fairly on the air.

(d) *Artistic Considerations.* The entertainment side of radio is also a topic which comes in for its share of criticism. By this is not meant the differences in program tastes which have already been discussed. Rather, the issue here is one of a general level of artistry... Dramatic and musical programs can be, for example, good or poor according to objective criteria. It is this aesthetic level of achievement that is often criticized by experts in the field. Such standards may actually be quite independent of the degree to which the audience enjoys a program.

Radio shares this problem with all commercialized arts and crafts. A few decades ago it was a general complaint that few people in America read books or had a chance to see a legitimate theater performance. Now book clubs distribute books by the millions, and an increasing number of theatrical companies are successfully touring the country. As a result of these broadened opportunities, the present-day complaint has turned to the fact that tastes in reading and drama are on a low level.[9]

9. John K. Hutchens, "For Better or Worse, the Book Clubs," *The New York Times Book Review*, Sunday, March 31, 1946, p. 1.

It is quite inevitable that as the market for the fine arts expands, its product becomes less subtle. This might be the price that is paid in a democratic society in order to achieve the largest possible participation of all people in all spheres of life. The beauty of Mozart's music was perhaps related to the fact that he wrote for only a small select group of listeners. Similarly, it might turn out that after some time there will be superimposed upon this phenomenon of mass culture a more restricted production of modern music or sophisticated drama which will lead a trend back to higher standards.

The art of literary criticism has itself undergone an interesting development in recent decades. There is a growing feeling that the soundest criticism does not come from frustrated journalists and poets who substitute their artistic ideas for the content of the piece that they are criticizing.[10] It is rather increasingly felt that the social conditions under which a piece of art is produced and the psychological conditions under which it is received constitute more legitimate data for literary criticism. In this connection there is great need to see such cultural and psychological insights applied to modern media of mass culture such as radio.[11]

One special aspect of this whole problem is the effect of radio programs on people's standards of conduct. Movies are credited with greatly influencing the lives of their audiences. Everything from crimes to coiffures have, at one time or another, been attributed to the effects of the motion picture. Strong claims of this sort are seldom made for radio, but some radio programs do have an influence on the listeners' daily lives. Daytime serials and children's programs, for example, are programs which sometimes have such effects.

---

10. For discussions along these lines see: Max Eastman, *The Literary Mind, Its Place in an Age of Science*, New York: Charles Scribner's Sons, 1931; and I. A. Richards, *Principles of Literary Criticism*, New York: Harcourt, Brace and Company, 1928.

11. For amplification see Leo Lowenthal, "Biographies in Popular Magazines," in *Radio Research, 1942-1943* by Paul F. Lazarsfeld and Frank N. Stanton, New York: Duell, Sloan and Pearce, 1944.

With regard to programs specifically aimed at children, the problem which radio faces is similar to and as difficult as that posed by children's books and comics.[12] Several years ago children's radio programs were under fire to such an extent that broadcasters became discouraged, with the result that the amount of time devoted to young people on the air was greatly decreased. At best, children's programs are likely to have small audiences and therefore are a greater commercial risk. Furthermore, the advertiser has to be especially careful in preparing a program and sales talk addressed to young people. The main problem seems to be whether it is possible to satisfy the desires of young people for adventure and at the same time give them some worthwhile personal standards. An experiment at combining entertainment and educational value is at present being conducted on the *Superman* program.[13] It is interweaving the "cliff-hanging technique" with crusades against intolerance in terms which children can understand. The success of the *Superman* experiment is being watched with interest.

(e) *The Problem of Social Significance.* Some critics feel that radio should exercise more leadership in progressive thinking on some of the larger social issues which face our time. At a time when so many divergent philosophies contend with one another, can it be asked of a single institution such as radio to take on the task of choosing among them? When a subject has very definitely become a national issue, and only then, can radio serve in its dissemination. An examination of radio schedules would show, for example, that in matters of racial and religious tolerance and cooperation, which are now being high-lighted, radio is contributed to the cause. And during the

---

12. The beginnings of standards for children's programs have been worked out by Howard Rowland, I. Keith Tyler and Norman Woelfel in *Criteria for Children's Radio Programs*, Columbus, Ohio: Evaluation of School Broadcasts, Ohio State University, 1942.
13. William B. Lewis, "Reformers Challenged by Superman," *Broadcasting*, May 13, 1946, p. 75.

war when a national goal was clear and delimited, the radio stations did a job which is widely acknowledged. The present survey asked the question:

> "*Taking everything into consideration, which one of these do you think did the best job of serving the public during the war—magazines, newspapers, moving pictures or radio broadcasting?*"

Sixty-seven per cent put radio on the top of the list with newspapers getting 17 per cent, magazines 3 per cent and moving pictures 4 per cent of the vote.

These then are the five areas of contention in the current radio discussion: advertising, educational duties of radio, freedom of the air, artistic standards, and the social significance of the current program schedules. In all of them the broadcaster has to mediate conflicting interests and points of views or he has to search ever new solutions for tasks which are, in the last analysis, of a creative nature. This leaves one question still to be discussed. All human beings are fallible; even the licensees of radio frequencies. How should we make sure that the industry, irrespective of individual failings, follows the best possible road?

Areas of Ignorance

In almost all spheres of business and public life, a modern democracy is faced with a serious and complicated problem. We cherish our individual liberties. But at the same time, large sectors of this country's activities are carried through by centralized organizations and rather long range planning. However much we should like to, philosophically, we cannot let each railroad engineer run his train according to the dictates of his conscience. How to attain the utmost individual freedom in a country where large scale economic and governmental organizations have become indispensable, is one of the great challenges of our time. In some areas the problem is not so noticeable. There have long been local laws which prohibited bakers from selling bread which is short in weight, and thus it was no great step to a Federal Trade Commission to supervise the veracity of advertising claims. In other spheres the problems are more complex and varied. When in the early 20's, large religious bodies objected to the output of the movie industry, a strong movement developed toward policing the content of films. After several years of public agitation, the movie producers and distributors organized a strong trade association which has set up and carried through a considerable amount of self-regulation.

As radio entered the national scene, the problem took still another form. For obvious reasons it is necessary to have public regulation of frequencies, power and similar technical details of radio operation. As a result radio has grown up with two regulatory bodies. The Federal Communications Commission takes care of the technical policing of this sort. But it is also vital to the public interest to have certain standards of programming and advertising. The industry itself has made the National Association of Broadcasters the guardian of the cultural and business standards which prevail and has given it the task of mediating between the interests of the individual broadcaster and public demands which are voiced by a variety of interest groups.

It is not surprising that frequent discussions arise as to the line at which self-regulation of the industry ends and government regulation begins. Can we appeal to the average citizen for a decision if problems develop in this borderline area?

For the time being the answer is probably no. The public looks at radio largely from the standpoint of the listener and is too little aware of the administrative problems involved. The present survey asked the question:

"*As far as you know, does the government have anything to do with the operation of radio stations?*"

Only 50 per cent of the cross-section said it did, 16 per cent said no, and 34 per cent said they did not know. It is in itself puzzling that only half of the population has even a rudimentary picture of how radio is organized in this country. The matter becomes still more significant when it is found that the very groups who listen to the radio most are the least informed. Women listen more because many of them are available during the day, and the lower educated strata listen more than the higher ones. Table 28 shows that information about government control of radio flows in quite the opposite direction.

Table 28

INFORMATION ON ROLE OF GOVERNMENT
IN OPERATION OF RADIO STATIONS
ACCORDING TO SEX AND EDUCATION

Government has a role?	MEN		WOMEN	
	HS graduation or more	Less than HS graduation	HS graduation or more	Less than HS graduation
Yes	79%	53%	52%	29%
No	11	17	17	19
Don't know	10	30	31	52
Total	100%	100%	100%	100%

Seventy-nine per cent of the men who have at least completed high school know that the government plays some role in the operation of radio stations, but only 29 per cent of the women in the lower educated group have the equivalent knowledge.[14]

14. It is an amusing coincidence that in this case education and sex compensate each other. The lower educated men are as well informed as the higher educated women. That women, by and large, are less informed than

The same high degree of ignorance emerges in a number of other questions asked in the present survey. It is impossible to ask people about any given situation if they are unaware of possible alternatives. In the case of the organization of radio, people do not even seem to know that any other alternative way of running radio actually exists. Only 22 per cent were aware that England has a different system.[15] It is true that 82 per cent know that the money to run radio stations in this country comes from advertising. And when asked how much of a radio station's time is sold, more than six out of ten answered correctly that half to three-quarters is sold. But only half of these knew that what the trade calls sustaining programs have to be paid for by the stations or the networks.[16]

The Role of the Government

Under such circumstances people cannot be expected to have clearcut ideas as to what the most desirable system of radio in this country would be. It is, therefore, more to provide a base against which to check opinion trends that the present survey asked a number of questions centering around the problem of public administration *vs.* commercial sponsorship of broadcasting, a problem which so excites the experts and with which people are so little concerned.[17]

The matter was approached in two different ways. First, a general question was asked:

---

men is a very general phenomenon of American life which deserves much more attention than it usually gets. But this is not the place to elaborate on this subject.

15. Descriptions of the British system of broadcasting control may be found in: Terence H. O'Brien, *British Experiments in Public Ownership and Control*, New York: Norton, 1938; William A. Robson, *Public Enterprise: Developments in Social Ownership and Control in Great Britain*, Chicago: University of Chicago Press, 1937; and Lincoln Gordon, *The Public Corporation in Great Britain*, New York: Oxford University Press, 1938.

16. See Appendix B, Questions 16, 18 and 19.

17. The questions hereafter reported were asked in a supplementary survey made with a smaller cross-section of people. For details see Appendix C.

"*Which do you think would be better for the people in this country—if the (each industry below) were run by the government, or by private business?*"

To have a reasonable comparison, five industries were cited: banks, coal mines, radio stations, newspapers and gas and electric companies. Table 29 shows that in these general terms, the people vote in all five cases for private business rather than for government.

Table 29

PUBLIC OPINION ON GOVERMNENT VS. PRIVATE CONTROL OF FIVE INDUSTRIES

	Coal mines	Banks	Gas and eleccric	Radio stations	News-papers
Government	40%	33%	30%	16%	10%
Private business	47	54	58	70	83
No opinion	13	13	12	14	7
Total	100%	100%	100%	100%	100%

People are relatively most inclined to favor public ownership of coal mines; banks and utilities run a close second. In the case of the two communications industries, radio stations and newspapers, the overwhelming vote is for private ownership.

Here again, incidentally, social stratification plays a very important role. The people in the lower stratum, the ones who have never gone beyond grade school, are two or three times as inclined to favor public ownership as are those in the highest stratum, who have gone to college.

The general willingness to have an institution such as radio run by private business can be expressed, so to speak, in dollars and cents. One question in the survey read:

"Would it be worth it to you to pay a tax of $5.00 a year to get radio programs without any advertising in them?"

Only 20 per cent are so willing. When the ante was raised to $10 a year, this figure drops to 7 per cent; and when people were asked if they would pay a tax of $25 a year, only 1 per cent says yes.[18]

But the answers reported in Table 29 probably reflect only a vague reaction to private ownership. When the problem is approached in a more specific way, people give completely different answers. It would hardly be fair to say that they contradict themselves. What happens is that they seem to lack a clearly reasoned picture of the problem, and from whatever direction they look at it, it seems different to them. The respondents in this survey were given a list of nine points at which government regulation of the radio industry could be possible. Three of them were of a technical nature and are now actually under FCC regulation. The other six are now left to the discretion of the stations. Each person in the sample was asked:

"Which of these powers do you think the federal government should have over radio?"

The items and the distribution of the answers are given in Table 30. For the purpose of this presentation, the items are divided into two groups: those the government is already regulating, and those which they do not now regulate.

The replies are curious in many respects. While only 15

18. The Princeton Radio Research Project asked the following question in a cross-section of a New Jersey town in 1938: "Most of the European countries do not have advertising on the radio. This is, of course, only possible where a country asks each owner of a radio to pay a license fee in order to cover expenses for programs that are here sponsored by certain companies. How much would you be willing to pay each month in order to have the programs you have now without the advertising?" Only 22 per cent were willing to pay a fee at all. Cf. Jeanette Sayre, "A Comparison of Three Indices of Attitudes Toward Radio Advertising," *Journal of Applied Psychology*, Vol. XXIII, No. 1, February, 1939, pp. 23-33.

per cent of the respondents want the government to "run radio," nevertheless up to two-thirds are willing to give it important powers. The three regulatory powers of the Commission which are considered necessary by all experts (frequency, wattage, and ownership) are less frequently approved than two others which the Communications Act does not now specifically cover: the truthfulness of news broadcasters, and the balanced presentation of public issues.

Table 30

PROPORTION WHO THINK THE GOVERNMENT SHOULD HAVE SPECIFIC POWERS OVER RADIO STATIONS[a]

	Per cent thinking the government should[b]
Give each station a regular place on the dial	45%
Tell each station how much power it can use	35
Approve of changes in ownership of stations	21
See to it that news broadcasts are truthful	66
See that radio stations regularly carry programs giving both sides of public issues	53
Make sure that each station broadcasts a certain number of educational programs	40
Decide how much time may be used for advertising	27
Limit the profits of radio stations	23
Decide what kinds of programs are to be broadcast	17

[a] People were also asked which functions the government actually does have. See Appendix B, Question 28, and Appendix C.
[b] Figures add to more than 100% because more than one answer per person was possible.

THE CRITIC, THE PEOPLE AND THE INDUSTRY   89

It is worthwhile to dwell for a moment on the details of Table 30. The desire for government regulation is perhaps an index of the importance with which people imbue an issue. From this point of view it appears clear that the man on the street is most sensitive to honesty on the air. As a matter of fact, one could put it this way. The question under discussion forces the respondent to make a choice between two cherished American stereotypes: fairness and free enterprise. If the two should be in conflict, the majority of the respondents give fairness priority. But in this connection it should be recalled that the public gives present day radio a very high rating on the issue of fairness.

Table 30 shows that most people are not very concerned with the limitation of profits or with changes in ownership of stations. Three other items are especially interesting in the light of our previous discussion. Considerably more people are interested in getting educational programs than the number who want the time for advertising limited. And at one point Tables 29 and 30 are very consistent. Only 15 per cent of the respondents want the government to run the radio; only 17 per cent want it to decide what kind of programs are to be broadcast.[19]

This last item suggests that the whole situation could be viewed from still another aspect. So far, it has been argued that this whole area of inquiry is not now an appropriate topic for a public opinion poll. People have little information on the subject; they have obviously given it little thought. And yet the results add up to an approval of exactly the type of system we have in this country. People do not want the government to run radio. They want it left in the hands of private industry,

19. The educational differences in the replies to the items of Table 30 are quite revealing. As far as non-technical items go, there is hardly any difference in the attitudes of educated and uneducated people. In regard to the three technical items, the educated people are more likely to want the government to have regulatory powers. Obviously, the educated strata are more aware of the administrative necessity for such regulation. For details see Appendix D, Table 28.

where indeed it is. But they are also aware of the power which such a system puts in the hands of commercial companies; and as good Americans, when they see power somewhere, they look at once for checks and balances. They feel that business institutions should be complemented by a government, which watches to see that the public gets a square deal. Should the industry to which they have entrusted their airways not keep faith with them, the government should see to their interests.

In a rather broad interpretation then, it can be said that the people leave it to the experts to determine the best delineation between self-regulation and government supervision. They want to look at the results. As long as industry plays fair they are willing to leave it alone. But they would certainly turn to the government if their distrust were aroused.

This survey has shown in a variety of ways that people are, by and large, satisfied with what American radio does for them. Still the progressive elements in the radio industry are only too right to be sensitive to the critics, especially to ask for criticisms as they have done in this survey. Radio, which reaches the ears of all the people, seems to have listened well to their voices. People say radio is fine; they want it to develop ever more so.

APPENDICES

Appendix A   CHARACTERISTICS OF
              THE SAMPLE

The National Opinion Research Center of the University of Denver which made this survey at the request of the National Association of Broadcasters is an academic institution working under grants from the Field Foundation and the University of Denver. It used its own national staff of personally trained interviewers scattered throughout the United States. The 2,571 personal interviews made for this study in November, 1945, represent a cross-section of the U.S. adult population. Well-established laws of probable error indicate that this number of interviews are accurate within about 3 per cent of true opinion. In other words, similar results would be obtained in 997 surveys out of any 1,000 conducted under comparable conditions.

In addition to this national cross-section of 2,571 interviews, an expanded sample of 672 people living in the Mountain and Pacific areas was included in order that geographic regions could be compared, the normal proportion of people living in those areas being too small for the reliable calculation of regional differences. These extra interviews were not, however, included in any of the calculations except where regional groups were shown.

The characteristics of the people interviewed with and without radios is shown in the tables which follow.

Appendix Table 1
SCOPE OF SAMPLE

Total Persons Interviewed		3243
Main Sample		2571
Total with radios in working order	2246	
Total without working radios	325	

(Table Continued on p. 94.)

SCOPE OF SAMPLE—*Continued*

Expanded Sample	672
(In Mountain and Pacific time zones only.)	
Total with radios in working order	616
Total without working radios	56

Appendix Table 2

CHARACTERISTICS OF THE SAMPLE

	TOTAL SAMPLE		RADIO HOMES	
	Number	Per cent	Number	Per cent
Total persons interviewed	2571	100%	2246	100%
Sex				
Men	1142	44%	984	44%
Women	1428	56	1261	56
Not ascertained	1		1	
Age				
Under 40	1053	41%	941	42%
40 to 59	1059	42	957	43
60 and over	418	17	338	15
Not ascertained	41		10	
Economic Level				
A (Wealthy)	43	2%	42	2%
B (Prosperous)	310	12	302	13
C (Middle class)	1431	56	1340	60
D (Poor)	787	30	562	25

CHARACTERISTICS OF THE SAMPLE—Continued

	TOTAL SAMPLE		RADIO HOMES	
	Number	Per cent	Number	Per cent
Educational Level				
Completed college	187	7%	180	8%
Some college	245	10	236	11
Completed high school	609	24	588	26
Some high school	484	19	435	19
Completed grade school	514	20	445	20
Some grade school	480	19	331	15
No schooling	38	1	20	1
Not ascertained	14		11	
Size of Community				
500,000 and over	515	20%	476	21%
100,000 to 500,000	495	19	443	20
25,000 to 100,000	386	15	320	14
2,500 to 25,000	349	14	331	15
Under 2,500	396	15	331	15
Farm	430	17	345	15
Geographic Region				
Northeast	728	28%	667	30%
Middle West	759	30	705	31
South	755	29	569	25
West	329	13	305	14

RADIO OWNERSHIP

The present study found 91 per cent of the population owning radios when interviewing was done in November, 1945. This figure is corroborated by the most recent analysis of the NAB Research Department which estimated 90 per cent of American homes to have radios as of January, 1946.

Appendix Table 3
RADIO OWNERSHIP

	Per cent
Do you have a radio in working order?	
Total with radios in working order	87%
Total with radios not working	4
Total owning radios	91%
Total without radios	9
Number of radios in home	
Five	1%
Four	2
Three	7
Two	26
One	54
None	9
Number not ascertained	1
Is there a car radio?	
Yes	24%
No	76
Is there an FM radio?	
Yes	3%
No	88
No radio	9
100% = total persons interviewed	2571
Age of radio most frequently used	
16 years or more	3%
13 to 15 years	5
11 to 12 years	4
9 to 10 years	15
7 to 8 years	18
5 to 6 years	31
3 to 4 years	15
2 years or less	2
Age of radio not ascertained	7
100% = total radio owners	2246

AMOUNT OF RADIO LISTENING

The amount of radio listening was ascertained in this survey by asking the following questions:

"On an average weekday, about how many hours do you listen to the radio during the daytime—that is, before 6 o'clock in the evening?"

"And on an average weekday, about how many hours do you listen to the radio after 6 o'clock in the evening?"

The range of hours that the people interviewed in this survey said they normally listen to the radio may be seen in Appendix B, questions 9 and 10.

The average amount of daytime listening was 2.3 hours, and average evening listening 2.6 hours. The differences between men and women's listening in the daytime, of course, presents a different picture. This may be seen in Appendix Table 4.

Appendix Table 4

AVERAGE HOURS OF RADIO LISTENING DAY AND EVENING COMPARED FOR MEN AND WOMEN

	Men	Women	Total
Average hours of daytime radio listening	1.3	3.0	2.3
Average hours of evening radio listening	2.3	2.9	2.6

Amount of radio listening also varies somewhat with age, educational level, size of town, and geographic region. These listening variations may be seen for evening radio listening in Appendix Table 5.

Appendix Table 5

AVERAGE HOURS OF EVENING RADIO LISTENING IN VARIOUS POPULATION GROUPS

		Average hours
Total radio owners		2.6
Educational level		
College		2.4
High school		2.6
Grammar school		2.7
Sex and Age		
Men	Under 40	2.5
	40 and over	2.2
Women	Under 40	3.1
	40 and over	2.7
Region		
East		2.6
Middle West		2.8
South		2.3
West		2.8
Size of community		
500,000 and over		2.8
100,000–500,000		2.9
25,000–100,000		2.6
2,500–25,000		2.5
Rural		2.3

Appendix B   QUESTIONNAIRE AND RESULTS

Questions 1 to 3 were asked of all persons interviewed.
100% = 2571

Ques. 1. A. *Do you have a radio in working order?*
B. *Do you usually read a daily newspaper?*
C. *Do you usually read a weekly newspaper?*
D. *Do you read any magazines regularly?*

	Working radio	Daily newspaper	Weekly newspaper	Magazines
Yes	87%	84%	35%	53%
No	13	16	65	47

100% = 2571

Ques. 2. *Taking everything into consideration, which one of these do you think did the best job of serving the public during the war—magazines, newspapers, moving pictures, or radio broadcasting?*

Magazines	3%
Newspapers	17
Moving pictures	4
Radio broadcasting	67
No opinion	9

100% = 2571

Ques. 3. *In every community, the schools, the newspapers, the local government, each has a different job to do. Around here, would you say that the schools are doing an excellent, good, fair or poor job? How about the newspapers? The radio stations? The local government? The churches?*

	Schools	Newspapers	Radio stations	Local government	Churches
Excellent	17%	12%	28%	7%	25%
Good	45	56	54	38	51
Fair	18	21	10	29	12
Poor	5	4	1	9	2
Don't know	15	7	7	17	10

100% = 2571

Questions 4 to 30 were asked of radio owners only.
100% = 2246

Ques. 4. A. *From which one source do you get most of your daily news about what is going on—the newspapers or the radio?*
B. *Which one gives you the latest news most quickly—the newspapers or the radio?*
C. *Which one gives you the most complete news—the newspapers or the radio?*
D. *And which one gives you the fairest, most unbiased news—the newspapers or the radio?*

	A. Most daily news	B. Latest news	C. Most complete news	D. Fairest news
Newspapers	35%	4%	67%	16%
Radio	61	94	27	57
Don't know	4	2	6	27

100% = 2246

Ques. 5. *In what ways do you think radio news could be improved?*^a

Less advertising	10%
More detailed news, longer broadcasts	9
Less opinion, more facts	7
Less repetition	4
More accurate, less premature news	3
Better presentation	3
More frequent news	3
Less restriction on news presentation	2
Requests for specific types of news	2
Miscellaneous suggestions	3
No criticisms, news is good as it is	29
No opinion	31
	100% = 2246

Ques. 6. *As far as your own listening is concerned, is the radio giving too much time, about the right amount, or not enough time to . . .*

	A. News about other countries	B. News about this country	C. News about things around here
Too much	10%	2%	2%
About right	64	66	57
Not enough	17	27	33
Don't know	9	5	8
	100% = 2246		

Ques. 7. *If you had to give up either going to the movies or listening to the radio, which one would you give up?*

Movies	84%
Radio	11
Don't know	5
	100% = 2246

^aMore than one answer per person was possible.

Ques. 8. *If you had to give up either reading the newspapers or listening to the radio, which one would you give up?*

        Newspapers   62%
        Radio   30
        Don't know   8

                100% = 2246

Ques. 9. *On an average weekday, about how many hours do you listen to the radio during the daytime—that is, before 6 o'clock in the evening?*

Ques. 10. *And on an average weekday, about how many hours do you listen to the radio after 6 o'clock in the evening?*

	Daytime	Evening
Over 6 hours	8%	*%
Over 5 to 6 hours	4	2
Over 4 to 5 hours	4	8
Over 3 to 4 hours	8	17
Over 2 to 3 hours	10	22
Over 1 to 2 hours	15	26
31 to 60 minutes	17	15
16 to 30 minutes	11	4
Up to 15 minutes	4	1
None, don't listen	18	4
No opinion	1	*
100% =	2246	2246

*Less than half of one per cent.

Ques. 11. A. *Here's a set of cards listing different kinds of radio programs. Would you mind looking through these cards, and telling me the types of programs you like to listen to in the daytime?*[a]

Ques. 11. B. *Now which types of programs there do you like to listen to in the evening?*[a]

	A. DAYTIME		B. EVENING
	Men	Women	Total
News broadcasts	65%	76%	76%
Radio plays	12	31	54
Comedy programs	14	25	54
Quiz programs	12	22	53
Old familiar music	24	40	47
Popular and dance music	15	35	42
Talks or discussions about public issues	22	21	40
Classical music	12	23	32
Sports events	28	13	27
Religious broadcasts	19	35	20
Serial dramas	7	37	11
Talks on farming	13	12	8
Children's programs	5	20	6
Home-making programs	6	44	5
Live stock and grain reports	14	6	4
Total radio listeners	984	1261	2246

[a] More than one answer per person was possible.

Ques. 12. *Are there any* kinds *of radio programs that aren't on when you'd like to listen to them?*

Ques. 13. *Are there any* kinds *of programs you'd like to hear* more *of?*

Ques. 14. *Are there any* kinds *of programs you'd like to hear* fewer *of?*

	Not on at right time	Like more	Like fewer
Yes	19%	41%	45%
No	81	59	55
	100% = 2246		

What Kinds?[a]

	Not on at right time	Like more	Like fewer
Drama			
Serial stories	1%	1%	16%
Mystery stories	*	1	4
Radio theater	1	3	*
Other drama	*	*	*
Music			
Popular	2	3	6
Familiar	1	3	2
Classical	3	8	2
Other music	1	2	*
Advertising	—	—	3
Comedy and variety	2	3	2
Children's programs	*	*	2
Quiz programs	*	2	2
Sports	1	1	1
Serious information programs	1	4	1
News programs	2	2	1
Religious programs	2	4	1
Farm programs	*	1	*
Women's programs	*	1	*
	100% = 2246		

[a] More than one answer per person was possible.
* Less than half of one per cent.

APPENDIX B

Ques. 15. *Aside from news, in what other fields does the radio add to your information or knowledge?*[a]

		Per cent
General knowledge		67%
Politics, current events, or history	22%	
Quiz programs	15	
Religion	5	
Science or medicine	4	
Art or literature	2	
Vocabulary or diction	2	
Geography, travel	2	
Broader view	2	
Miscellaneous	3	
General, everything	10	
Practical information		31%
Home-making	19%	
Agriculture	9	
Advertising or shopping information	3	
Enjoyment or cultural information		25%
Music	16%	
Drama	5	
Sports	4	
Don't learn from radio or listen only for entertainment		25%
	100% =	2246

[a] More than one answer per person was possible.

Ques. 16. *As far as you know, is the radio broadcasting in England run any differently from the way it is here?*

Yes	22%
No, no difference	11
Don't know	67
	100% = 2246

A. IF "YES": *What is the main difference?*[a]

No advertising	8%
Government control	6
Paid for by tax	2
Less advertising	2
Programs are inferior	2
More censorship or politics	1
Programs are superior	1
Miscellaneous	2
Don't know	2
	100% = 2246

[a] More than one answer per person was possible.

Ques. 17. *Do you ever feel like criticizing when you listen to the radio?*

        Yes   64
        No[a]   36

            100% = 2246

A. IF "YES": *What are some of your main criticisms? Any others?*[b]

Advertising		29%
Too much advertising	15%	
Silly advertising	4	
Advertising interrupts	3	
Singing commercials	3	
Repetitiousness	2	
False advertising	2	
Objections to product	1	
Contents of talks or news		13%
Disagree with viewpoint	6%	
Political talks	2	
Miscellaneous	6	
Voice, delivery or talent		7%
Comic or silly aspects		4
Daytime serials		4
Asocial aspects of programs		3
Jazz music		3
Bad taste in jokes or slang		2
Classical music		1
Miscellaneous		4

            100% = 2246

[a] Including no answer to the question.
[b] More than one answer per person was possible.

Ques. 18. *As far as you know, where do radio stations get the money to run them?*[a]

Advertising, or sponsors	82%
Government, or taxes	2
The public, individuals	2
Networks or station owners	1
Political parties	1
Religious, charitable organizations	1
Other	2
Don't know, no answer	13 |//
100% =	2246

[a] More than one answer per person was possible.

Ques. 19. *As you know, every radio station broadcasts many different programs each day. About how many of these programs would you say are sold to advertisers—all of them, about three-quarters of them, about half of them, about one quarter, or less than that?*

All are sold	20%
Three-quarters	53
Half are sold	11
One-quarter	1
Less than one-quarter	*
Don't know	15

100% = 2246

A. UNLESS "ALL" OR "DON'T KNOW": *Who pays for the programs broadcast during the rest of the time?*[a]

Stations, or networks	31%
Profits from advertising	3
Government, or taxes	4
Political parties	2
Religious, charitable organizations	4
The public, individual donations	3
Other sources	4
Don't know, no answer	21

100% = 2246

*Less than half of one per cent.
[a]More than one answer per person was possible.

Ques. 20. A. *If your newspaper could be produced without advertising, would you prefer it that way?*

B. *If your radio programs could be produced without advertising, would you prefer it that way?*

	A. Newspaper	B. Radio
Yes	10%	35%
No	87	62
Don't know	3	3
	100% = 2246	

C. *Those who wanted advertising in newspapers but not on the radio were asked informally why their answers were different.*[a]

You can skip ads in the paper, radio forces you to listen	7%
Prefer products and type of local information given in newspapers	6
Radio advertising takes too much time	5
Radio advertising interrupts program	5
Prefer visual presentation	3
Radio advertising repetitious	3
Listen to radio for entertainment	2
Radio advertising far-fetched	1
Miscellaneous	1
No opinion	1
	26% = 579

[a] More than one answer per person was possible.

Ques. 21. *Which one of these four statements comes closest to what you yourself think about advertising on the radio?*

    A. I'm in favor of advertising on the radio, because it tells me about the things I want to buy.   23%
    B. I don't particularly mind advertising on the radio. It doesn't interfere too much with my enjoyment of the programs.   41
    C. I don't like the advertising on radio, but I'll put up with it.   26
    D. I think all advertising should be taken off the radio   7
    No opinion   3

                                      100% = 2246

Ques. 22. *Would it be worth it to you to pay a tax of $5 a year to get radio programs without any advertising in them?*

    A. IF "YES": *Would it be worth a tax of $10 a year?*

    B. IF "YES" TO "A": *Would it be worth a tax of $25 a year?*

    Would pay:
        $25 a year   1%
        $10 a year but not $25   6
        $5 a year but not $10   13

    Total would pay   20%
    Would not pay $5 a year   80

                                        100% = 2246

Ques. 23. *Can you give an example of what you think is the best advertising you've heard on the radio?*

    A. IF "YES": *What did you like about it?*[a]

Ques. 24. *Can you give me an example of what you think is the worst advertising you've heard on the radio?*

    A. IF "YES": *What didn't you like about it?*[a]

	Liked	Disliked
Could give me no example[b]	57%	61%
Gave example	43	39
	100% = 2246	

	Liked	Disliked
Singing or rhyming commercials	5%	11%
Variety *vs.* monotony	3	7
Brevity *vs.* lengthiness	10	6
Clever *vs.* silly humor	8	4
Unbiased *vs.* biased	2	4
Dignity *vs.* poor taste	2	4
Identifying slogans or sound effects	1	3
Fits program *vs.* interrupts	10	2
Manner or voice of announcer	3	2
Instructive *vs.* useless	4	*
Miscellaneous	5	4
	100% = 2246	

[a] More than one answer per person was possible.
[b] Including no answer to the question.
*Less than half of one per cent.

APPENDIX B

Ques. 25. *Here are some criticisms of radio advertising or commercials. Would you tell me which ones, if any, you feel strongly about?*[a]

Interrupts programs	35%
Claim too much for product	33
Too repetitious	32
Silly	31
Too long	30
Too many of them	26
Too many jingles	18
Too much singing	15
Too detailed	13
Bad taste	13
Don't feel strongly about any	27
	100% = 2246

Ques. 26. *Are there any products listed here which you think should not be advertised over the radio?*[a]

Whiskey	42%
Beer	36
Liver remedies	22
Laxatives	20
Headache remedies	16
Cigarettes	12
Deodorants	11
Gasoline	5
Tooth paste	5
Bread	4
Ice cream	4
Automobiles	4
All should be allowed to advertise	49
	100% = 2246

[a] More than one answer per person was possible.

Ques. 27. *Do you think that radio stations should sell time for the following things, or should they give the time free, or shouldn't they be on the air at all? How about . . .*

	Sell	Give	Not on air	No opinion	Total
1. Political broadcasts	76%	7%	9%	8%	100%
2. To solicit correspondence school registrations	60	9	15	16	100
3. To solicit members for business men's organizations	57	6	21	16	100
4. To solicit labor union memberships	42	7	36	15	100
5. To solicit funds for churches	13	57	22	8	100
6. To solicit Community Chest donations	8	78	6	8	100
7. To solicit Red Cross memberships	8	82	4	6	100

100% = 2246

APPENDIX B

Ques. 28. *As far as you know, does the government have anything to do with the operation of radio stations?*

Yes	50%
No	16
Don't know	34
	100% = 2246

A. (IF "YES") *As far as you know, which of these powers does the Federal government have over radio stations?*[a]

B. (ASKED OF EVERYONE) *Which of those powers do you think the Federal government should have over radio stations?*[a]

	A. Does	B. Should
Give each station a regular place on the dial	69%	45%
Tell each station how much power it can use	63	35
Approve of changes in ownership of stations	31	21
See to it that news broadcasts are truthful	31	66
See that radio stations regularly carry programs giving both sides of public issues	23	53
Make sure that each station broadcasts a certain number of educational programs	26	40
Decide how much time may be used for advertising	14	27
Limit the profits of radio stations	14	23
Decide what kinds of programs are to be broadcast	11	17
100%[b] =	387	1091

[a] More than one answer per person was possible.
[b] The figures shown here are taken from the Supplementary Sample III. For a detailed explanation see Appendix C.

Ques. 29. *As far as you know, does the government require radio stations to broadcast a certain number of religious and educational programs, or do the stations broadcast these voluntarily?*

>   Government requires   4%
>   Do it voluntarily   62
>   No opinion   34
>
>   100% = 2246

Ques. 30. *I'd like to ask you how fair you think radio stations, newspapers and magazines generally are. For example, do you think radio stations are generally fair in giving both sides of an argument? How about newspapers in general? Magazines?*

	Radio stations	Newspapers	Magazines
Yes	81%	39%	45%
No	8	49	22
No opinion	11	12	33

>   100% = 2246

Appendix C SUPPLEMENTARY SAMPLES

Two supplementary surveys were taken after the first sample of 2246 radio homes. The second survey was made principally to refine some of the statements in the first; parts

Appendix Table 1
STRATIFICATION OF THREE SAMPLES INTERVIEWED

RADIO HOMES

	Sample I	Sample II	Sample III
Sex			
Male	44%	43%	48%
Female	56	57	52
Economic Level			
Prosperous	15%	16%	14%
Average	60	55	57
Poor	25	29	29
Education			
College	19%	16%	16%
High school	45	44	47
Grammar school	36	40	37
Age			
Under 40	45%	42%	45%
40 and over	55	58	55
Size of Town			
100,000 and over	41%	57%	43%
2500 to 100,000	29	14	28
Under 2500 and farm	30	29	29
Total in each sample	2246	498	985

117

of the questions concerned with program types and with what people learn from radio were re-worded. The third survey was made because of an oversight in the first. In the first survey, only those people who had known that the government does have something to do with the operation of radio stations were asked the question, "Which of these powers do you think the government should have over radio stations?" The third questionnaire remedied this by asking the latter question of the entire sample. The three samples are highly comparable with respect to stratification.

The fact that the three samples are so similar in the characteristics which influence their responses to a questionnaire of this type justifies our use of all three as representative.

The three samples can be compared also with respect to their answers to two questions: "Does the government have anything to do with the operation of radio stations?"

Appendix Table 2

INFORMATION CONCERNING THE ROLE OF GOVERNMENT IN THE OPERATION OF RADIO STATIONS FOR SAMPLES I, II AND III

Government plays a role:	Sample I	Sample II	Sample III
Yes	50%	39%	35%
No	16	25	31
Don't know	34	36	34
Total radio listeners	2246	498	1091

There is a discrepancy in the extent of information among those in the first sample, as compared with the second and third, for which we are unable to account. However, the sex

Appendix Table 3

INFORMATION ON ROLE OF GOVERNMENT IN OPERATION OF RADIO STATIONS BY SEX AND EDUCATION, SAMPLE II

Government plays a role:	MEN		WOMEN	
	High school graduation or more	Less than high school graduation	High school graduation or more	Less than high school graduation
Yes	70%	44%	38%	21%
No	18	25	36	22
Don't know	12	31	26	57
Total radio listeners[a]	71	140	117	166

[a] Four cases are omitted from the total of 498 because they had given no answer to this question.

Appendix Table 4

INFORMATION ON ROLE OF GOVERNMENT IN OPERATION OF RADIO STATIONS BY SEX AND EDUCATION, SAMPLE III

Government plays a role:	MEN		WOMEN	
	High school graduation or more	Less than high school graduation	High school graduation or more	Less than high school graduation
Yes	63%	33%	41%	19%
No	25	35	27	34
Don't know	12	32	32	47
Total radio listeners	190	328	211	362

and educational differences found on this question are decidedly confirmed in the two supplementary surveys. Compare the table shown in the text for the first sample on page 52 with Appendix Tables 3 and 4 on page 119.

The same results are striking in all three samples: Men are much better informed than women, and the more educated are much better informed than the less educated.

Appendix Table 5

ATTITUDES OF LISTENERS FROM SAMPLES I, II AND III WHO KNOW GOVERNMENT PLAYS ROLE IN RADIO

The government should:	Sample I	Sample II	Sample III
Give each station a regular place on the dial	54%	60%	65%
Approve of changes in ownership of stations	35	34	34
Tell each station how much power it can use	52	56	57
See to it that news broadcasts are truthful	69	53	68
Decide how much time may used for advertising	22	37	33
Decide what kinds of programs are to be broadcast	24	32	20
Limit the profits of radio stations	27	21	27
Total radio listeners who know the government plays a role in radio	1129	192	395

The three samples are also comparable on the question which asked, "Which of these powers do you think the government should have over radio stations?" See Table 5. The proportion wanting government regulation in all three samples is fairly similar for each item in the list.

Appendix D APPENDIX TABLES

Appendix Table 1A

PROPORTION WHO FEEL ANNOYANCE AT RADIO ADVERTISING BY GENERAL ATTITUDE TOWARD ADVERTISING

	ATTITUDE TOWARD ADVERTISING			
	In favor	Don't mind	Put up with	Take off air
Feel annoyed at advertising	21%	27%	52%	64%
Total radio listeners	520	919	590	155

The proportion who spontaneously mention that they feel annoyed at radio advertising increases as each step in the general question reflects a more negative attitude toward ad-

Appendix Table 1B

PROPORTION WITH FIVE OR MORE CRITICISMS OF COMMERCIALS BY GENERAL ATTITUDE TOWARD ADVERTISING

	ATTITUDE TOWARD ADVERTISING			
	In favor	Don't mind	Put up with	Take off air
Five or more criticisms	5%	10%	26%	48%
No criticisms	42	28	10	5
Total radio listeners	520	919	590	155

vertising. As in the table shown in the text, we note that there is a marked difference between those who "don't mind" advertising and those who "put up with" it. Here, 25 per cent more of the latter group than of the former spontaneously mentioned annoyance at advertising.

Appendix Table 2

TWO ATTITUDES TOWARD RADIO
BY GENERAL ATTITUDE TOWARD ADVERTISING

	ATTITUDE TOWARD ADVERTISING			
	In favor	Don't mind	Put up with	Take off air
Learned from radio[a]				
General knowledge	60%	71%	68%	79%
Practical information	43	30	26	17
Enjoyment or culture	24	23	30	30
Don't learn or listen only for entertainment	21	25	23	26
Radio's job in community:				
Excellent	39%	29%	25%	24%
Good	53	59	55	52
Fair	5	9	16	16
Poor	1	*	2	5
Don't know	2	3	2	3
Total radio listeners	520	919	590	155

[a] More than one answer per person was possible.
*Less than half of one per cent.

Appendix Table 3

INFLUENCE OF SPECIFIC DISSATISFACTIONS WITH RADIO ON OVERALL APPRAISAL OF RADIO AS AN INSTITUTION

Dissatisfactions:	JUDGMENT OF RADIO					Rating of Radio[a]	100% = Total radio listeners
	Excellent	Good	Fair	Poor	Don't know		
"Do you ever feel like criticizing when you listen to the radio?"							
Feel annoyed	30%	54%	12%	2%	2%	2.98	1427
Do not feel annoyed	30	58	7	*	5	3.11	808
"Are there any kinds of programs you'd like to hear more of?"							
Want more	30%	54%	12%	2%	2%	2.98	931
Do not want more	30	56	9	1	4	3.05	1315
"Are there any kinds of programs you'd like to hear fewer of?"							
Want fewer	29%	55%	12%	2%	2%	2.97	1018
Do not want fewer	30	56	9	1	4	3.05	1228

[a]This score is devised by giving each "institution" 4 points for every respondent who calls it "excellent"; 0 points for everyone who calls it "poor"; the judgment "good" is worth 3 points; and "fair" takes 1 point. People who answer "don't know" are given the benefit of the doubt and rated 2 points each.
*Less than half of one per cent.

INFLUENCE OF SPECIFIC DISSATISFACTIONS WITH RADIO ON OVERALL APPRAISAL OF RADIO AS AN INSTITUTION—Continued

Dissatisfactions:	JUDGMENT OF RADIO					Rating of Radio[a]	100% = Total radio listeners
	Excellent	Good	Fair	Poor	Don't know		
"Are there any kinds of programs that aren't on when you'd like to listen to them?"							
Dissatisfied	30%	54%	12%	2%	2%	2.98	430
Satisfied	30	56	10	1	3	3.04	1816
"As far as your own listening is concerned, is radio giving too much time, about the right amount, or not enough time to:							
News about things around here							
Dissatisfied	30%	53%	14%	2%	1%	2.95	778
Satisfied	31	57	9	1	2	3.07	1291
News about other countries							
Dissatisfied	28%	55%	13%	2%	2%	2.95	615
Satisfied	32	56	9	1	2	3.09	1433
News about this country							
Dissatisfied	34%	50%	12%	2%	2%	3.02	655
Satisfied	29	58	10	1	2	3.04	1483

[a] This score is devised by giving each "institution" 4 points for every respondent who calls it "excellent"; 0 points for everyone who calls it "poor"; the judgment "good" is worth 3 points; and "fair" takes 1 point. People who answer "don't know" are given the benefit of the doubt and rated 2 points each.

Appendix Table 4
PRODUCTS CONSIDERED UNSUITABLE FOR RADIO BY EDUCATION, SEX AND SIZE OF COMMUNITY[a]

	HIGH SCHOOL GRADUATION OR MORE			LESS THAN HIGH SCHOOL GRADUATION		
	Cities 100,000 and over	Towns 2,500 to 100,000	Rural under 2,500	Cities 100,000 and over	Towns 2,500 to 100,000	Rural under 2,500
MEN						
Whiskey	33%	33%	33%	43%	39%	47%
Beer	26	26	23	37	31	45
Liver remedies	40	24	17	19	20	16
Laxatives	30	23	16	15	15	19
Headache remedies	27	19	14	14	13	12
Cigarettes	13	9	5	14	12	16
Deodorants	19	13	10	7	7	9
Gasoline	6	4	2	7	5	6
Tooth paste	7	5	3	4	5	5
Bread	6	4	2	7	5	4
Ice cream	6	1	2	5	4	6
Automobiles	4	2	1	6	5	4
All should be allowed to advertise	48%	56%	58%	50%	54%	50%
Total men radio listeners	172	141	111	229	149	179

[a] More than one answer per person was possible.

PRODUCTS CONSIDERED UNSUITABLE FOR RADIO BY EDUCATION, SEX AND SIZE OF COMMUNITY[a]—Continued

	HIGH SCHOOL GRADUATION OR MORE			LESS THAN HIGH SCHOOL GRADUATION		
	Cities 100,000 and over	Towns 2,500 to 100,000	Rural under 2,500	Cities 100,000 and over	Towns 2,500 to 100,000	Rural under 2,500
			WOMEN			
Whiskey	35%	35%	55%	36%	45%	65%
Beer	27	30	51	28	36	59
Liver remedies	29	24	28	19	7	16
Laxatives	26	22	30	15	8	15
Headache remedies	22	16	20	13	7	10
Cigarettes	9	11	18	9	11	16
Deodorants	15	10	19	9	3	12
Gasoline	4	1	5	5	2	7
Tooth paste	4	3	6	3	2	7
Bread	4	1	4	4	1	5
Ice cream	3	1	3	4	2	5
Automobiles	3	1	3	3	1	7
All should be allowed to advertise	50%	49%	34%	56%	51%	32%
Total women radio listeners	224	184	172	289	173	211

[a] More than one answer per person was possible.

SEVERITY OF CRITICISM

The list of criticisms in Table 12 in the text also gives a manageable index of each respondent's attitude toward commercials. Counting the number of criticisms each person checked, it is found that 27 per cent have no objections, 30 per cent have one or two objections, 28 per cent three or four, and 15 per cent five or more. Now there exists an old rule in all areas of persuasion to the effect that if one wants to win over opponents, one should not begin with the most critical ones. It is easier to persuade the milder critics than

Appendix Table 5
CRITICISMS OF ADVERTISING BY NUMBER OF CRITICISMS CHECKED[a]

	NUMBER OF CRITICISMS		
Criticism of advertising	One or two	Three or four	Five or more
Too long	21%	44%	71%
Bad taste	6	15	47
Too detailed	4	16	48
Too much singing	7	17	53
Too repetitious	19	49	80
Interrupt programs	28	51	77
Silly	20	43	81
Jingles	7	21	61
Claim too much for product	29	48	72
Too many	16	34	72
Total radio listeners	693	620	346

[a] More than one answer per person was possible.

the main antagonists. It will not be easy for a radio station or an advertiser, however willing he is, to please people who feel that everything is wrong with advertising and who therefore check practically every item in such a list of possible criticisms. He will probably be much more likely to come to terms with people who check only a few items.

To suggest an answer, all the respondents who expressed some criticism were divided into three groups: those who checked only one or two items, those who checked three or four items, and those who checked five items or more. These three groups of critics for purposes of classification may be termed "lenient," "moderate," and "severe." In Appendix Table 5 they are compared for the type of complaint they mentioned most frequently.

When a comparison is made of the three types of critics as to their answers in the four-step scale of attitudes toward advertising, the results are shown in the following table:

Appendix Table 6

GENERAL ATTITUDE TOWARD ADVERTISING
BY NUMBER OF CRITICISMS CHECKED

	NUMBER OF CRITICISMS			
Attitude toward advertising	No criticisms	One or two	Three or four	Five or more
In favor	37%	25%	17%	7%
Don't mind	45	45	41	26
Put up with	11	24	34	43
Off the air	1	5	7	21
Don't know	6	1	1	3
Total radio listeners	587	693	620	346

It can be seen that when the people who are against advertising are considered (those who "put up" with advertising and those who think it should be off the air), 29 per cent of the "lenient" critics, 41 per cent of the "moderate" critics, and 64 per cent of the "severe" critics take the negative side.

But it can be seen from Appendix Table 5 that the resulting groups of critics are not strictly comparable. Every item was checked much more by the "severe" critics than by the "lenient" critics, which is, of course, a result of the way these three groups have been classified. Among the lenient critics, the average item was checked by 23 per cent; among the moderate critics an average of 55 per cent checked each complaint; while among the severe critics, 67 per cent checked the average item in the basic list.

In order to make these different types of critics comparable —to know whether the "lenient" critics stress different items relative to the "severe" critics, index figures are used. The three groups just mentioned are equated by calling the average of each 100. If, then, for the "lenient" critics an item is picked out by 31 per cent of the people, this would be about one-third more than their average (23%) and would receive the index 135. The "moderate" critics would furnish such an index number if an item were criticized by 74 per cent of all the people, which is again about one-third more than the average of 55.

According to the index numbers so obtained the objections to advertising cluster into three groups. The first is composed of items on which the "lenient" critics feel relatively stronger than the "severe" critics. Next come the complaints which are relatively stronger with the "severe" critics. Finally, at the end of the list are the criticisms which are of about equal weight for all three groups.

There are three items which are relatively most frequent among the "lenient" critics. These are the objections that commercials are too long, interrupt the program and claim too much for the product. The complaints which are stressed relatively more often by the "severe" critics than by the "lenient" are: bad taste, too detailed, too much singing, too many jingles.

In other words, translating this result again into the five

Appendix Table 7

INDEX OF CRITICISM OF RADIO COMMERCIALS

	LENIENT CRITICS (1 or 2 criticisms)	MODERATE CRITICS (3 or 4 criticisms)	SEVERE CRITICS (5 or more criticisms)
Criticisms Strongest with Lenient Critics			
Claim too much for product	185	140	110
Interrupt programs	178	151	116
Too long	134	133	107
Criticisms Strongest with Severe Critics			
Bad taste	38	44	71
Too detailed	25	47	71
Too many jingles	45	62	92
Too much singing	45	50	80
Criticisms Showing Little Difference			
Silly	127	127	122
Too repetitious	121	145	121
Too many of them	102	101	110
Average index	100	100	100
Average proportion of checkmarks	23%	55%	67%
Total radio listeners	693	620	346

basic factors already discussed, the "lenient" critics object especially to the volume and position of commercials and the tendency to oversell. These are the two factors which the industry, by self-regulation, should do something about in rather short order.

This is, in a way, a fortunate result. Of the five main psychological factors which have been shown to lead to antagonism, these are the two which the broadcaster's can do something about. Let them begin at this point. Experience has shown that good will created among mild opponents is likely to spread to the more bitter antagonists. If commercials were shorter and not so often placed in the middle of the program, and if intense and often exaggerated claims were modified, a considerable forward step would have been accomplished.

PROGRAM PREFERENCES

Appendix Table 8

PROGRAM PREFERENCES FOR DAYTIME AND EVENING BY SEX[a]

	DAYTIME		EVENING		
	Men	Women	Men	Women	Total
News broadcasts	65%	76%	79%	74%	76%
Radio plays	12	31	44	62	54
Comedy programs	14	25	52	55	54
Quiz programs	12	22	50	55	53
Old familiar music	24	40	47	48	47
Popular and dance music	15	35	38	45	42
Talks or discussions about public issues	22	21	47	35	40
Classical music	12	23	28	36	32
Sports events	28	13	43	14	27
Religious broadcasts	19	35	19	20	20
Serial dramas	7	37	9	14	11
Talks on farming	13	12	12	5	8
Children's programs	5	20	4	7	6
Home-making programs	6	44	3	7	5
Live stock and grain reports	14	6	8	1	4
Total radio listeners	984	1261	984	1261	2246

[a] More than one answer per person was possible.

Because of some inadequacy and ambiguity in the above list of radio programs, a similar question was inserted in a supplementary small nation-wide ballot on which interviewing was done in March, 1946. The two major changes in the list were:

(1) Insertion of audience participation programs (programs other than quiz in which ordinary people are brought into the studio), and
(2) A finer definition of "radio plays" and "serial dramas" thus—"complete radio plays" and "continued serial stories".

The results are shown in Appendix Table 9 on page 135.

The chief differences from Table 8 are the following:

(1) Audience participation programs rank in the bottom half of people's program preferences for both daytime and night-time programs.
(2) The proportion liking serial stories did not vary greatly with the more defined statement. But the proportion mentioning "radio plays" in the daytime decreased markedly when it was clearly understood that "complete radio plays" was meant. In other words, previous confusion between "radio plays" and "serials" seems to have been to some extent eliminated.
(3) There is evidence that preference for news programs declined somewhat from the first survey in November, 1945, to March, 1946. It is still the highest in rank, but the proportion mentioning news dropped from 76 to 70 per cent in the five intervening months. While these figures are not conclusive, it is possible that there is some let-down in news interest as the end of the war recedes into the distance.

Appendix Table 9

PROGRAM PREFERENCES FOR DAYTIME AND EVENING BY SEX[a]
(Supplementary Sample)[b]

	DAYTIME		EVENING		
	Men	Women	Men	Women	Total
News broadcasts	51%	65%	72%	68%	70%
Complete radio plays	7	23	33	46	40
Comedy programs	14	23	59	59	59
Quiz programs	6	18	49	53	51
Old familiar music	19	38	35	41	37
Popular and dance music	16	32	40	48	44
Talks or discussions about public issues	11	17	39	26	32
Classical music	10	17	24	26	25
Sports events	19	6	39	11	23
Programs (other than quiz) in which ordinary people are brought into the studio	6	21	20	23	22
Religious broadcasts	12	35	16	18	17
Continued serial stories	10	40	8	10	9
Talks on farming	9	13	7	2	4
Children's programs	3	15	2	6	4
Home-making programs	3	34	1	3	2
Live stock and grain reports	10	3	4	*	2
Total radio listeners	212	287	212	287	499

[a] More than one answer per person was possible.
[b] For details see Appendix C.
*Less than half of one per cent.

Appendix Table 10
EVENING PROGRAM PREFERENCES BY EDUCATION AND BY AGE[a]

	EDUCATION			AGE			
	College	High school	Grammar school	20–29	30–39	40–49	50 and over
News broadcasts	76%	77%	75%	69%	76%	78%	78%
Radio plays	51	59	49	62	61	55	44
Comedy programs	53	58	49	62	59	56	44
Quiz programs	57	57	45	53	53	54	52
Old familiar music	49	45	50	39	45	47	54
Popular and dance music	40	49	34	72	50	41	22
Talks or discussions about public issues	55	40	33	28	38	43	46
Classical music	54	32	21	34	28	32	34
Sports events	30	29	21	29	28	29	23
Religious broadcasts	12	17	27	11	16	16	29
Serial dramas	7	14	11	14	12	11	10
Talks on farming	6	7	10	4	7	8	11
Children's programs	4	6	7	5	8	6	5
Home-making programs	4	5	6	4	4	5	6
Live stock and grain reports	3	3	7	2	4	4	6
Total radio listeners	416	1023	796	384	557	554	741

[a] More than one answer per person was possible.

Appendix Table 11

EVENING PROGRAM PREFERENCES BY SIZE OF TOWN AND BY REGION[a]

	SIZE OF TOWN			REGION			
	Cities 100,000 and over	Towns 2,500 to 100,000	Rural under 2,500 and farm	North East	Mid-west	South	West
News broadcasts	78%	74%	76%	75%	75%	79%	76%
Radio plays	60	54	46	54	57	48	55
Comedy programs	59	53	48	57	56	47	58
Quiz programs	50	55	55	50	50	56	55
Old familiar music	48	45	49	53	44	45	55
Popular and dance music	44	43	38	46	41	43	40
Talks or discussions about public issues	39	45	38	43	36	35	49
Classical music	37	35	24	43	28	21	37
Sports events	31	28	20	29	25	22	30
Religious broadcasts	17	20	23	15	15	28	25
Serial dramas	14	8	10	12	10	11	11
Talks on farming	5	5	14	5	9	10	9
Children's programs	6	6	7	6	5	7	7
Home-making programs	5	5	6	5	4	5	5
Live stock and grain reports	3	3	8	3	4	6	6
Total radio listeners	919	651	676	667	705	569	921

[a] More than one answer per person was possible.

Appendix Table 12

WOMEN'S DAYTIME PROGRAM PREFERENCES BY EDUCATION AND BY AGE[a]

	EDUCATION			AGE			
	College	High school	Grammar school	20–29	30–39	40–49	50 and over
News broadcasts	72%	78%	75%	73%	79%	74%	75%
Home-making programs	35	45	48	43	47	47	42
Old familiar music	37	37	45	34	40	37	47
Serial dramas	26	38	41	42	40	38	30
Popular and dance music	29	38	33	53	40	35	17
Religious broadcasts	22	30	49	26	30	36	46
Radio plays	26	32	34	34	33	28	30
Comedy programs	19	28	22	30	29	24	17
Classical music	33	24	16	26	23	20	21
Quiz programs	17	22	25	21	20	21	26
Talks or discussions about public issues	24	22	18	16	23	22	22
Children's programs	15	21	21	22	27	17	15
Sports events	12	17	9	16	14	16	9
Talks on farming	9	11	15	5	12	14	15
Live stock and grain reports	2	6	8	3	6	6	8
Total radio listeners	212	630	411	262	334	298	361

[a] More than one answer per person was possible.

Appendix Table 13

WOMEN'S DAYTIME PROGRAM PREFERENCES BY SIZE OF TOWN AND BY REGION[a]

	SIZE OF TOWN			REGION			
	Cities 100,000 and over	Towns 2,500 to 100,000	Rural under 2,500 and farm	North East	Mid-west	South	West
News broadcasts	74%	75%	78%	67%	78%	82%	76%
Home-making programs	40	42	52	38	48	48	43
Old familiar music	37	38	45	38	41	39	43
Serial dramas	39	35	36	34	41	40	28
Popular and dance music	39	35	28	34	38	34	28
Religious broadcasts	30	32	45	23	37	49	29
Radio plays	35	28	30	28	31	36	32
Comedy programs	29	21	22	21	26	27	23
Classical music	27	23	18	26	23	17	26
Quiz programs	22	22	23	18	24	24	24
Talks or discussions about public issues	20	21	22	19	23	19	26
Children's programs	19	18	23	18	19	22	24
Sports events	14	13	12	8	17	12	18
Talks on farming	7	8	21	6	16	12	13
Live stock and grain reports	4	4	11	4	9	4	8
Total women radio listeners	517	359	385	370	399	324	168

[a] More than one answer per person was possible.

Appendix Table 14
EVENING PROGRAM PREFERENCES BY EDUCATION AND SIZE OF TOWN[a]

	COLLEGE			HIGH SCHOOL			GRAMMAR SCHOOL		
	Cities	Towns	Rural	Cities	Towns	Rural	Cities	Towns	Rural
News broadcasts	80%	71%	78%	79%	74%	77%	77%	74%	74%
Radio plays	54	50	49	66	57	50	55	51	39
Comedy programs	57	48	53	61	58	53	57	48	39
Quiz programs	51	63	60	53	58	61	47	43	44
Old familiar music	49	50	50	47	40	47	50	49	51
Popular and dance music	42	41	38	54	48	43	35	37	31
Talks or discussions about public issues	57	56	50	38	43	41	31	40	29
Classical music	62	50	49	35	35	24	29	22	12
Sports events	34	35	19	34	29	24	26	21	15
Religious broadcasts	7	11	21	15	17	20	25	29	27
Serial dramas	9	4	7	19	10	12	12	8	10
Talks on farming	4	6	11	4	4	13	6	7	18
Children's programs	4	4	5	5	6	6	7	6	8
Home-making programs	3	6	5	4	5	5	6	5	7
Live stock and grain reports	2	3	4	2	3	6	4	3	12
Total radio listeners	164	139	111	403	317	303	346	191	259

[a] The size of town is: Cities 100,000 and over; Towns 2500 to 100,000; Rural under 2500 and farm. More than one answer possible per person.

Appendix Table 15

EVENTNG PROGRAM PREFERENCES BY AGE AND EDUCATION[a]

	21–29 YEARS			30–39 YEARS			40–49 YEARS			50 AND OVER		
	C.	H.S.	G.S.	C.	H.S.	G.S.	C.	H.S.	G.S.	C.	H.S.	G.S.
News broadcasts	64%	71%	65%	81%	79%	69%	76%	81%	76%	77%	78%	79%
Radio plays	64	64	46	57	64	58	52	59	50	38	45	45
Comedy programs	63	63	56	58	61	54	54	59	53	42	43	45
Quiz programs	58	53	40	56	58	41	53	59	46	61	57	47
Old familiar music	47	38	35	50	42	47	43	48	47	56	54	54
Popular and dance music	70	72	71	48	54	43	40	41	41	19	21	23
Talks or discussions about public issues	41	28	13	56	38	24	57	45	31	59	53	39
Classical music	67	30	13	48	26	18	53	33	18	54	40	25
Sports events	36	28	29	27	31	20	28	32	25	31	25	19
Religious broadcasts	8	11	13	12	15	19	9	16	22	16	28	33
Serial dramas	11	17	6	6	14	13	7	10	15	6	14	9
Talks on farming	6	3	4	5	8	7	2	9	11	11	8	12
Children's programs	3	5	6	7	9	8	4	5	8	2	3	7
Home-making programs	3	3	8	4	5	4	4	5	6	5	6	6
Live stock, grain reports	2	2	4	4	3	4	1	4	6	4	4	8
Total radio listeners	64	266	52	113	291	152	116	258	177	122	201	413

[a] C. means college, H.S. means high school, G.S. means grammar school. More than one answer per person was possible.

Appendix Table 16
SOURCE OF MOST DAILY NEWS BY SEX AND EDUCATION

	MEN			WOMEN		
	College	High school	Grammar school	College	High school	Grammar school
Newspaper	59%	42%	34%	39%	32%	22%
Radio	39	55	62	56	64	72
No preference	2	3	4	5	4	6
Total radio listeners	204	392	385	212	630	411

Appendix Table 17

CRITICISMS OF TIME GIVEN TO NEWS ABOUT OTHER COUNTRIES BY TIME GIVEN TO NEWS ABOUT THINGS AROUND HERE

	FOREIGN NEWS		
LOCAL NEWS	Too much	About right	Not enough
Too much	2%	1%	3%
About right	43	66	46
Not enough	48	28	47
No opinion	7	5	4
Total radio listeners	218	1433	397

Reference to Appendix D, Table 8, will show that in the total population the following proportions checked each type of music as their favorite in the evening:

Old familiar music	47%
Popular and dance music	42
Classical music	32

These figures do not, however, show the total proportion liking to listen to all kinds of music, since many people checked more than one of these three types. Altogether 76 per cent indicated that they liked some kind of music. The proportions checking each combination of two or three types of music, those checking only one kind, and those checking none are shown in the following table:

Appendix Table 18

PROPORTION LIKING DIFFERENT COMBINATIONS OF MUSICAL TYPES

Combinations of music tastes	Per cent
All three:	
Familiar, popular and classical	9%
Two types:	
Familiar and popular	12
Familiar and classical	10
Popular and classical	6
Only one type:	
Familiar music	16
Popular music	15
Classical music	8
Total liking to listen to any music	76%
No music preferences	24
Total radio listeners	2246

Appendix Table 19

DIFFERENCES BETWEEN WOMEN SERIAL AND NON-SERIAL LISTENERS IN RADIO-MINDEDNESS BY EDUCATION

	HIGH SCHOOL GRADUATION OR MORE		LESS THAN HIGH SCHOOL GRADUATION	
	Serial listeners	Non-serial listeners	Serial listeners	Non-serial listeners
From which source do you get most of your daily news:				
Newspapers	23%	42%	20%	28%
Radio	74	53	74	68
No preference	3	5	6	4
Usual amount of evening radio listening:				
Less than 2 hours	35%	49%	34%	46%
2 or 3 hours	53	40	47	43
4 or more hours	12	11	19	11
Usual amount of daytime radio listening:				
Not at all	—%	20%	—%	15%
Less than 2 hours	15	34	11	24
2 or 3 hours	26	28	28	31
4 or more hours	57	16	61	29
No answer	2	2	—	1
Total women radio listeners	175	405	288	385

Appendix Table 20

EXAMPLES OF PROGRAMS CONSIDERED SERIOUS OR EDUCATIONAL[a,b]

	Per cent
Forums	21%
Quiz programs	16
Religious programs	8
Farm programs	4
Classes on the air	3
Crime programs	3
Classical music programs	3
Home-making and shopping programs	3
Advice and psychology programs	3
Stories	3
Children's programs	1
Miscellaneous	17
Don't know or no answer	28
Total radio listeners	498

[a] More than one answer per person was possible.
[b] This question was asked of one of the supplementary samples which are explained in detail in Appendix C.

Appendix Table 21

NUMBER OF RADIO LISTENERS BY AGE, SEX AND EDUCATION

	HIGH SCHOOL GRADUATION OR MORE		LESS THAN HIGH SCHOOL GRADUATION	
	Men	Women	Men	Women
Under 40	182	333	161	261
40 and over	239	244	385	405

Appendix Table 22

PROPORTION LIKING TO LISTEN TO RELIGIOUS PROGRAMS IN THE EVENING BY SIZE OF TOWN AND EDUCATION[a]

	College	High school	Grammar school
Cities 100,000 and over	7%	15%	25%
Towns 2,500 to 100,000	11	17	29
Under 2,500 and farm	21	20	27

[a] See also Appendix D, Table 14.

Appendix Table 23

WHAT PEOPLE ON DIFFERENT EDUCATIONAL LEVELS WANT TO HEAR MORE OF ON THE RADIO

	College	High school	Grammar school
Music			
Classical	16%	8%	4%
Familiar	2	3	4
Popular	2	4	1
Other	2	3	2
Drama	5	6	5
Comedy and variety	2	3	4
Information	8	4	2
Quiz programs	2	1	2
Religion	3	2	8
News	3	2	2
Sports	1	2	1
Other	2	3	3
Don't learn	52	59	62
Total radio listeners	416	1023	795

Appendix Table 24

ECONOMIC LEVEL OF PEOPLE WITH COLLEGE, HIGH SCHOOL AND GRAMMAR SCHOOL EDUCATION

	EDUCATION		
Economic level	College	High school	Grammar school
High (A and B)	41%	13%	4%
Intermediate (C)	52	66	46
Low (D)	7	21	50
Total persons interviewed	432	1083	1032

Appendix Table 25

AVERAGE NUMBER OF FAVORITE EVENING PROGRAMS BY EDUCATION AND AMOUNT OF EVENING LISTENING

	AMOUNT OF EVENING LISTENING			
	Up to 1 hour	1 to 2 hours	2 to 3 hours	3 or more hours
College	4.4	5.1	5.7	5.7
High school	3.9	4.9	5.6	5.5
Grammar school	3.7	4.3	5.3	5.5

Appendix Table 25A

NUMBER OF PERSONS IN EACH BOX

AMOUNT OF EVENING LISTENING

	Non-listeners	Up to 1 hour	1 to 2 hours	2 to 3 hours	3 or more hours	Total
College	10	111	130	83	80	414
High school	29	177	256	241	317	1020
Grammar school	46	169	197	168	213	793
Total	85	457	583	492	610	2227[a]

[a] There were 19 radio owners whose education or radio listening was not ascertainable.

Appendix Table 26

INFORMATION LEARNED FROM THE RADIO BY PEOPLE IN TOWNS OF DIFFERENT SIZES[a]

Learn from radio:	Cities 100,000 and over	Towns 2,500 to 100,000	Villages under 2,500	Farms
General knowledge	65%	77%	61%	54%
Practical information	27	23	31	58
Enjoyment or cultural information	24	28	30	20
Don't learn or listen only for entertainment	26	22	27	21
Total radio listeners	918	651	331	345

[a] More than one answer per person was possible.

Appendix Table 27

USE MADE OF RADIO BY LISTENERS ON DIFFERENT EDUCATIONAL LEVELS[a]

	College	High school	Grammar school
News and entertainment only	35%	44%	52%
Some serious programs	55	51	38
Chiefly serious programs	8	5	5
No answer	2	*	5
Total radio listeners	78	217	202

[a] Asked of supplementary sample. See Appendix C.
*Less than half of one per cent.

Appendix Table 28

PROPORTION WHO THINK THE GOVERNMENT SHOULD HAVE POWERS OVER RADIO STATIONS BY EDUCATIONAL LEVEL[a]

The Government should:	High school graduation or more	Less than high school graduation
Give each station a regular place on the dial	55%	41%
Approve of changes in ownership of stations	25	18
Tell each station how much power it can use	43	30
See to it that news broadcasts are truthful	66	67
See that radio stations regularly carry programs giving both sides of public issues	56	51
Decide how much time may be used for advertising	29	25
Decide what kinds of programs are to be broadcast	16	17
Make sure that each station broadcasts a certain number of educational programs	41	39
Limit the profits of radio stations	20	25
Total persons interviewed	401	690

[a] More than one answer per person was possible.

INDEX

Advertising, aesthetic objections to, 30-36; amount of, 26-27, 35-37, 100-101, 106-107; and general attitude toward radio, 24-25, 118, 119; and government regulation, 88, 115, 119, 120; and human interest, 20-21; and tax on radio, 87, 111; approval of, 19-23, attention-getting devices, 31, 34, 37, 128, 131; attitudes toward, 13-37, 110-113, 122, 123, 128, 129, 131; bad taste in, 29, 34-35, 36-37, 112, 126, 127, 128, 131; beer, 29, 31, 35, 126, 127; CBS code on, 34; competition in, 32, 33; content of, 27-28, 33-34; criticisms of, 13-37, 67, 71, 107, 110-113, 122, 124, 128-135; deodorants, 30, 34, 126, 127; dramatized, 31, 34; entertainment value of, 28-29; frequency of, 26, 35, 36-37; good taste in, 29; headache remedy, 30, 34, 126, 127; history of radio, 13-15; improvement of, 32-37; informative value of, 21-23, 28, 105, 112; integration of, 27; interruptiveness of, 27, 32, 33, 36, 107, 110, 112, 128, 131; jingles, 31, 34, 36-37, 128, 131; laxative, 30, 34, 126, 127; learning from, 21-23, 123; length of, 26-27, 32-37, 110, 112, 128, 131; limitation of, 32; liquor, 29-31, 34, 126, 127; liver remedy, 30, 126, 127; medical, 29, 30, 34, 113, 126, 127; middle commercial, 33; NAB code on, 32; NBC code on, 34; newspaper, 14-15, 24, 33, 110; of organizations, 75-76; overselling, 28-29, 32-37, 110, 128, 131; position of, 26-27, 33, 35-36; products unsuitable for radio, 29-31, 34, 126, 127; proportion critical of, 17-20; repetitiousness of, 27, 31, 34, 36-37, 107, 110, 131; self-regulation of, 33-34, 132-134; singing commercials, 31, 36-37, 107, 112, 128, 131; soap, 28, 29, 31; whiskey, 29-31, 34, 126, 127

Age in relation to, popular music, 46-47, 48; program preferences, 49, 136, 138, 141; public affairs programs, 58-60; religious programs, 62-63

Age of radio sets, 96

Age of respondents, 94, 123

Agricultural programs, see Farm programs

Alcoholic beverages, 29-31, 34, 126, 127

American School of the Air, 53

Amount of radio listening, vii, 52, 97-98, 101-102

Appraisal of radio in general, 5-8; and amount of listening, 7-8; and attitude toward advertising, 24-25, 123, 124

Archer, Gleason, 13

Atkinson, Carroll, 53

Attention-getting devices, 31, 34, 37, 128, 131

Attitude, description of an, 15-20; measurement, 7

Attitudes among age groups, 46-49, 58-60, 62, 136, 138, 141

Attitudes among, educational groups, 43, 47, 51, 51-52, 58-60, 62-63, 66-68, 72, 86, 89-90, 119, 126, 127, 136, 138, 140, 141, 142, 145, 146, 147, 148, 149, 150, 151; geographic regions, 41, 49, 95, 98, 137, 139; men and women, 41, 43, 49-53, 58, 59, 103, 119, 126, 127, 133, 135, 138, 139, 142, 146, 147; urban and rural residents, 30, 41, 45, 47-48, 49, 56, 61-62, 95, 98, 137, 139, 140, 149

Attitudes toward, advertising, 13-37, 110-113, 122-123, 128, 129, 131; audience participation programs, 61-

153

62, 135; comedy programs, 45-46, 103, 103-104, 133-141, 147; forums, 58-59, 146; government regulations, 73-75, 86-90, 115, 116, 118-120; music programs, 46-49, 103, 104, 105, 133-141; news programs, 41-45, 103, 104, 133-141, 147, 149; quiz programs, 57, 58, 60-61, 103, 104, 133-141, 146, 147; religious programs, 57, 58, 62-64, 75, 103, 104, 116, 133-141, 146, 147; serial stories, 49-53, 103, 104, 133-141; tax on radio, 86-87, 111; whiskey advertising, 29-31, 34, 126, 127
Audience building, 11-12, 38-39
Audience participation programs, 61-62, 135
Audience ratings, 39-40
Automobile radios, 96

Bad taste in advertising, 29-30, 34, 36-37, 112, 126, 127, 128, 131
Beer advertising, 29-31, 34, 126, 127
Berelson, Bernard, 60
Blue network, 50
Book Clubs, 79-80
British radio, 11
Broadcast Music, Inc., 77
Broadcaster, role of, 69-71; social responsibility of, 33
Bryson, Lyman, 72
Bureau of Applied Social Research, vii
Business men's organizations, 75

Cantril, Hadley, 76
Car radios, 96
Cavalcade of America, 53
Chicago Round Table, 53
Children's programs, 81, 103, 104, 133-141, 146
Churches, 6-9, 75, 100
Cigarette advertising, 28, 30, 126, 127
Classical music, *see* Music
College people, tastes of, *see* Education
Columbia Broadcasting System, 34, 50
Columbia University, vii

Comedy Programs, 45-46, 103, 104, 133-141, 147
Commentators, 26, 42, 45, 76-77, 79
Commercials, *see* Advertising
Communications Act, 70
Community Chest, 75
Connah, Douglas D., 39
Criticisms of advertising, 13-37, 67, 71, 107, 110-113, 122-124, 128-131
Criticisms of radio, viii-ix, 9-12, 15-20, 51-52, 65-68, 75-78, 107
Critics, 38, 80-81
Cultural influence of radio, 49

Dance music, *see* Music
Daytime radio, 50-53, 61, 97, 102, 103, 133-135, 138-139, 145
Daytime serials, *see* Serials
Deodorants, 30, 34, 126, 127
Devotional programs, *see* Religious programs
Discussion programs, 11, 56-60, 103, 133-141, 146
Drama, 40, 49-53, 57, 79, 103, 104, 133-141, 147
Dramatized commercials, 31, 34

Eastman, Max, 80
Economic level of respondents, 94, 148
Education, influence on, amount of listening, 98, 145, 148; attitudes toward government regulations, 86, 88-90, 118-120, 151; classical music listening, 47; criticism of radio, 51, 66-68, 126, 127; knowledge, 84; learning from the radio, 72, 149; news listening, 43, 136, 138, 140, 141, 142, 145; program preferences, 136, 138, 140-141, 147, 148; public affairs programs, 58-60; religious programs listening, 62-64, 147; serial stories listening, 51, 136, 138, 140, 141, 145
Education of respondents, 94-95, 146
Education on the Air, 50, 55
Educational broadcasting, 11-12, 53-63, 71-73, 88, 116, 146, 151
English broadcasting, 11, 85, 106
Entertainment, 79-81, 149-150

Erdelyi, Michael, 11
Evening radio, 8, 47, 97, 102, 103, 133-137, 140-141, 145, 148-149

Familiar music, see Music
Farm programs, 21, 57, 103, 104, 133-141, 146
Federal Communications Commission, 53, 83, 87-88
Federal Trade Commission, 83
Fibber McGee and Molly, 27
Field Foundation, 93
FM, see Frequency modulation
Ford Hour, 29
Foreign news, 10, 44, 101, 125, 143
Forums, 58-60, 146
Freedom of speech, 73-79
Frequency modulation, 53-54, 56, 96

Gaudet, Hazel, vii, 60
Geographic region, 41, 49, 95, 98, 137, 139
Gordon, Lincoln, 85
Government, and education, 53-54, 151; local, compared with radio, 5-9, 100; regulation of radio, 14, 58, 73-75, 82-90, 115-116, 118-120
Guttman, Louis, 55

Headache remedy advertising, 30, 34, 126, 127
Herzog, Herta, 60
History of Radio, 13-15
Home-making programs, 21, 57, 103, 133-141, 146
Huges, Helen McGill, 21
Hutchens, John K., 80

Institute for Education by radio, 55
Interviews, number of, 93-95
Informative value of radio, 20-23, 57, 105, 112, 123, 149
Ivory Soap, 31

Jazz, see Music
Jingles, 31, 34, 36-37, 128, 131

Kansas Radio Audience of 1945, 41

Labor unions, 75

Landry, Robert J., 38
Lasswell, Harold D., 77
Laxative advertising, 30, 34, 126, 127
Learning from advertising, 20-23, 123
Learning from radio, 20-23, 53-64, 71-73, 123, 146, 149
Lewis, William B., 81
Life Magazine, 42, 76-77
Liquor advertising, 29-31, 34, 126, 127
Listening tastes determined by offerings, 10-12
Listeners to, comedy programs, 45-46; educational programs, 53-64; forums, 58-60; music, 46-49; news programs, 41-45; quiz programs, 60-62; religious programs, 62-64; serial stories, 49-53
Listening tastes, 38-64, 132-141
Listening to radio, amount of, vii, 52, 97-98, 102; and appraisal of radio, 7-8; and criticism, 9-11
Literary criticism, 80-81
Liver remedy advertising, 30, 126, 127
Livestock and grain reports, 103, 133-141
Local government, 5-9, 100
Local news, 44-45, 101, 124, 143
Look Magazine, 42
Lowenthal, Leo, 80

MacDougald, Duncan, Jr., 11
Magazines, 14, 38, 42, 73, 78-79, 82, 99
March of Time, 27
Market reports, 103, 133-141
Medical advertisements, 29-30, 34, 113, 126, 127
"Middle" commercial, 33
Minneapolis Star Journal, 6
Minnesota Poll, 6
Minority tastes, 3, 39, 69
Morgan, Henry, 38
Motion pictures, 80-82, 83, 99, 101
Murphy, Gardner, 7
Murphy, Lois, 7
Music, 11, 12, 46-49, 57, 79, 103, 104, 133-141; and age differences, 46, 47, 136, 138, 141; and educational

differences, 47, 48, 136, 138, 140, 141, 147; classical, 11, 12, 47-49, 63, 133-141, 143, 144, 146, 147; comparison of types, 143, 144; dance, *see* Music, popular; jazz, *see* Music, popular; old familiar, 49, 133-141, 143, 144, 147; popular, 11, 46-48, 49, 133-141, 143, 144, 147

National Association of Broadcasters, vii, ix, 32, 33, 77, 83, 93
National Broadcasting Company, 34, 35, 50
National Opinion Research Center, vii, 93
Networks, 13, 34, 35
Newcomb, Theodore, 7
News programs, 41-45, 103, 104, 105, 133-141, 147, 149; amount of listening to, 41-45; and advertising, 26, 27; and educational differences, 43, 136, 138, 140, 141, 142, 145; and newspapers, 42, 100, 142, 145; and sex differences, 43, 133, 135, 142; bias in, 44, 45, 76, 77, 88, 115, 120, 151; commentators, 26, 27, 42, 45, 76, 77, 79; composition of audience to, 41, 42, 133-141, 147; criticisms, 43-45, 67, 101; foreign news, 43, 44, 101, 125, 143; local news, 43, 44, 101, 125, 143; national news, 43, 44, 101, 125
Newspapers, 13, 74; advertising, 14, 15, 24, 33, 110; and radio news, 42, 100, 142, 145; and serial listeners, 52, 145; and urban readers, 21; compared with radio, 5-8, 38, 41, 42, 52, 78, 79, 82, 93, 99, 100, 101, 102, 110, 142; fairness of, 78, 79
Newsweek, 42
Number of interviews, 93, 94
Number of radios owned, 95, 96

O'Brien, Terence H., 85
Ohio State University, 50, 55, 81
Old familiar music, *see* Music

Participation programs, *see* Audience participation programs

Philharmonic broadcasts, 53
Place of residence of respondents, 95
Plays, 40, 103, 133-141
Political broadcasts, 57, 75
Popular music, *see* Music
Practical information on the radio, 20-22, 57, 123, 149
Princeton Radio Research Project, 87
Products objectionable on the air, 29-31, 34, 35, 126
Professor Quiz, 60
Program logs, 38
Program offerings, 11, 12
Program preferences, 11, 12, 38-64, 51, 52, 103, 133-141, 147
Program preferences of, age groups, 46-48, 59, 60, 62, 136, 138, 141; educational groups, 43, 47, 48, 51-52, 58-60, 62-64, 136, 138, 140, 141, 147; geographic regions, 41, 49, 137, 139; men and women, 41, 43, 59, 60, 103, 133, 135, 138, 139; urban-rural groups, 41, 45, 47, 48, 49, 56, 63, 65, 66, 137, 139, 140, 147
Program ratings, 39, 40
Public affairs programs, 57-60, 88, 103, 133-141, 151
Public opinion, limitations of, viii, 3-5, 31, 38, 70-71, 74-75, 76-77, 78, 89-90

Quiz programs, 57, 58, 60-62, 103, 104, 133-141, 146, 147

Racial tolerance, 81
Radio, advertising, 13-37; annoyance with, 8-12; appraisal of, 5-8, 24-26, 123, 124-125; audience, 38-39; compared with other institutions, 5-8; criteria for evaluating, 3-5; criticisms of, viii, ix, 9-12, 15-20, 51-52, 65-68, 75-78, 107, 124-125; critics, 38; fairness of, 76-79, 89; financing of, 13-15, 86-87, 108, 109, 111; entertainment value of, 79-81, 149, 150; history of, 13-15; impartiality of, 3; learning from, 20-23, 53-64, 71-73, 123-146, 149; news,

41-45, 52, 67, 77, 79, 100, 101, 115, 120, 133-143, 147, 150; regulation of, 14, 58, 73-74, 82-90, 98-102, 115-116, 118-120; social responsibility of, ix, 33; social significance of, 4, 5, 81-82; tax on, 14, 86-88, 111; uses of, 21, 54-55; war-time, 82, 99
Radio listening, amount of, vii, 52, 97-98, 101-102
Radio plays, 40, 133-141
Radio set ownership, 96
Radio stations, 78, 88, 108-109, 151
Ratings, program, 39-40
Red Cross, 75
Region, see Geographic region
Regulation of radio, 14, 58, 73-74, 82-90, 98-102, 115-116, 118-120
Religious programs, 57, 58, 62-64, 75, 103, 104, 116, 133-141, 146, 147
Research ideas, ix, 4, 12, 33, 44-45, 48-49, 55, 73, 76-77
Research on, advertising, 33; educational programs, 56, 73; freedom of speech, 76; music programs, 46-48; news programs, 44-45; program tastes, 47-48; supply and demand for programs, 11
Richards, I. A., 80
Robinson, Thomas Porter, 13
Robson, William A., 85
Roosevelt, President, 15
Roper, Elmo, 41
Rowland, Howard, 81
Rural listening, 41, 45, 47, 48, 49, 56, 63, 95, 98, 126, 127, 137, 139, 140, 147, 149

Sandage, C. H., 44
Satire, 45-46
Schools, advertising of, 34, 35; compared with radio, 5-8, 100
Serials, 10, 11, 35, 40, 49-53, 103, 104, 133-141; and amount of radio listening, 52; and audience participation shows, 61, 62; and education, 50-52, 136, 138, 140, 141, 145; and newspaper reading, 52, 145; and radio-mindedness, 51-53, 145; effects of, 80, 81

Serious broadcasts, see Educational broadcasting
Serious music, see Music
Sex differences, and amount of listening, vii, 97-98; and government regulation, 119; and news listening, 43, 133, 135, 142; and products suitable for advertising, 126-127; and program preferences, 40, 42-43, 59-60, 103, 133, 135, 138-139; and public affairs listening, 58-60
Siepmann, Charles A., 38
Singing commercials, 31, 36, 37, 107, 112, 128, 131
Smith, Jeannette Sayre, vii, 87
Soap advertising, 28, 29, 31
Social criticism, 46
Social institutions and radio, 5-8
Social responsibility of radio, ix, 33
Social significance of radio, 4-5, 81-82
Social stratification, 65-68, 86
Song plugging, 11
Sound effects in advertising, 31, 34, 37, 56, 113, 128, 131
Sponsored broadcasts, see Advertising
Sports programs, 57, 103, 104, 105, 133-141, 147
Stanton, Frank N., 11, 49, 50, 80
Subscription radio, 86-87
Suchman, Edward, 49
Superman Program, 81
Supplementary samples interviewed, 117-121
Sustaining programs, 22

Taboos, violation of in advertising, 29-35
Talks and discussions on public affairs, 12, 58-60, 103, 133-141, 146
Tax on radio, 14, 86-87, 111
Telephone ratings, 40
Time Magazine, 42
Tyler, I. Keith, 81

Unions, 75, 76
University of Denver, vii, 93
Urban listening, 30, 41, 45, 47, 49, 56, 61-62, 95, 98, 126-127, 137, 139, 140, 147, 149

U. S. Department of Agriculture, Bureau of Agricultural Economics, Division of Program Surveys, 47
Uses of radio, 21, 53-55

Variety programs, 45-46, 103, 104, 133-141, 147

Waples, Douglas, 77
Whan, F. L., 41

Whiskey advertising, 29-30, 34, 35, 126-127
Woefel, Norman, 81
Women, and amount of listening, vii, 97-98; and home-making information, 56, 57; and news listening, 41, 42-43, 133, 135, 142; and products suitable for advertising, 30, 126-127; and program preferences, 41, 42-43, 59-60, 103, 133, 135, 138-139; and serial stories, 49-53, 133, 135

www.ingramcontent.com/pod-product-compliance
Lightning Source LLC
Chambersburg PA
CBHW030114010526
44116CB00005B/237